INSIGHTS TO LITERATURE
Primary

by Judith Cochran

Incentive Publications, Inc.
Nashville, Tennessee

Cover by Susan Eaddy
Illustrated by Dianna Richey

ISBN 0-86530-191-3

Table of Contents

The Littles

Lafcadio, The Lion Who Shot Back

Ramona And Her Father

ABOUT THIS BOOK

INSIGHTS TO LITERATURE Primary is a literature and writing program designed to accompany 29 popular books for grades K-4. The books are divided into three groups:

Wordless Books – those books having rich illustrations with no written language in them.

Picture Books – those having pictures and a written story that is read in a single sitting.

Novels – chapter books.

Utilizing a whole language and thematic approach to teaching literature, this book ensures a higher range of comprehension, skills development, and appreciation for great literature.

Each piece of literature referenced in this book is presented through a learning unit comprising a Teacher's Guide, Activities, and Thematic Activities. Every Teacher's Guide contains pre/post reading discussion questions and activities and journal writing activities. The discussion questions/activities link the students' experiences to the story and touch upon all areas of the curriculum. Journal writing activities are organized by skill level (prewriters, beginning writers, and experienced writers).

All the questions and activities on the Activity pages and in the Teacher's Guides are correlated to Bloom's Taxonomy, with a particular emphasis on the upper levels requiring critical thinking. Each question and activity is marked with an abbreviation denoting the specific level it reinforces:

K = Knowledge

C = Comprehension

Ap = Application

An = Analysis

Sy = Synthesis

Ev = Evaluation

Thematic activities for math, science, social studies, fine arts, and language arts are provided.

Important reading skills are also reinforced in this program through the story activities. They are:

sequencing	making inferences	measuring
narrative writing	categorization	alphabetic principle
drawing conclusions	graphing	expository writing
summarizing	poetry	cause/effect relationships
letter form	predicting outcomes	story elements
guided imagery	descriptive words	mapping

INSIGHTS TO LITERATURE, K-4, can be easily implemented in any classroom program. With interest in literature on the rise, well-rounded literature/writing programs are sorely needed. INSIGHTS TO LITERATURE meets this need by offering a well-designed program based on the latest research, with an excellent balance between writing skills, critical thinking, and literary appreciation.

Wordless Books

ANNO'S ALPHABET

PREREADING DISCUSSION:

C What are some things that begin with the letter A, B, C, etc.? (List/draw on board).

This is an alphabet book with each letter made of wood. Look carefully at the shapes of the letters and remember any funny shapes. See which pictures are used for each one.

POSTREADING DISCUSSION:

C Did you see the way some of the letter shapes were different? Which letters were they? (Discuss.)

JOURNAL WRITING:

C/Ap **Group Activity** - What are some other things that begin with the letter A, B, C, etc.? (Add to prereading list on board.)

C/Ap **Prewriters** - Write down some letters and draw pictures to go with them. (Choose 2 or 3 of the letters being studied in class.)

C/Ap **Beginning Writers** - Write the letters in your first name. Draw pictures that start with the same letter as each letter in your name.

C/Ap **Experienced Writers** - Write your first and last name. Draw pictures and write words that start with the same letter as each letter in your name.

ANNO'S ALPHABET

C/AP
Prewriters

Write your name in the box.

Draw pictures to go with each letter in your name.

Name _____

ANNO'S ALPHABET

Sy
Beginning/Experienced Writers

Make your own alphabet book.

Reproduce this page and cut out the strips.

Staple the strips together to create your book pages.

Write a letter on each page.

Name _____

ANNO'S ALPHABET

MATH

GRAPHING:
Help your teacher graph the frequency of letters in names of children in your class.

SCIENCE

ALPHABET WALK:
Take a walk outside. Draw/write things you see that start with certain letters/sounds.

SOCIAL STUDIES

ALPHABET TOWN:
Draw a large map of a town with streets and locations marked to go with each letter of the alphabet. (Example: Alligator Alley, Big Baby Bowling, Cute Cat Corner, etc.)

FINE ARTS

COLLAGE:
Cut pictures from magazines that start with certain letters. Compile them into a class book.

LANGUAGE ARTS

BODY LANGUAGE:
When your teacher calls out letters or words, form your body into the first letter's shape. (This can be done with children in pairs and can be lots of fun.)

DEEP IN THE FOREST

PREREADING DISCUSSION:

 Think about the story of "The Three Bears." How does it go? (Fill in story frame on board).

Example:	WHO	WHERE	WHAT HAPPENED
Beginning Middle End	Papa Bear Mama Bear Baby Bear Goldilocks	Bears' house in forest	Bears went for a walk. Goldilocks came in house, etc.

This is a picture story about a little bear who does what Goldilocks did. See how this story is the same and different from "The Three Bears."

POSTREADING DISCUSSION:

 How was this story the same and different from "The Three Bears"? (Draw and list on board.)

Same	Different
_____	_____
_____	_____
_____	_____

JOURNAL WRITING:

 Group Activity - Write a story frame of the story. (Limit sections of story frame to "first" and "last" for prewriters.)

Example:	WHO	WHERE	WHAT HAPPENED
Beginning Middle End	Papa Mama Little girl Little Bear	House in woods	People went for walk. Little Bear gets in house, etc.

 Prewriters - Draw your own story frame of the first and last parts of the story.

 Beginning Writers - Draw and label your own story frame of the beginning, middle, and end of the story.

Experienced Writers - Write a story frame of what happens in the beginning, middle, and end of the story. Illustrate your story frame when finished.

DEEP IN THE FOREST

Color and cut out the puppet. Paste it on a paper bag and tell the story.

Name _____

DEEP IN THE FOREST

Make another cover for this book.

Name _____

DEEP IN THE FOREST

MATH

ADD 'EM UP:
Add up all the characters and important objects in the story.
Example: 3 bear cubs
            1 mama bear
            1 cabin
            3 bowls

CATEGORIZATION:
Draw pictures of characters/objects in story on cards. In small groups, categorize them in as many ways as possible.

SCIENCE

ALL ABOUT BEARS:
Learn about bears.

IN THE WOODS:
Learn about living in a cabin in the woods. What kinds of chores would children do? What would be the same/different from living where you live now?

SOCIAL STUDIES

POINT OF VIEW:
In small groups, retell "Deep In The Forest" from the bears' point of view and the little girl's point of view. Then retell "The Three Bears" from the bears' point of view and Goldilocks's point of view.

FINE ARTS

DIORAMA:
Construct dioramas of the story.

LANGUAGE ARTS

PUPPET SHOW:
In small groups, put on a puppet show of the story.

BOBO'S DREAM

PREREADING DISCUSSION:

Ap Have you ever had a dream in which you do things you can't do in real life? (Discuss.)

This is a story about a dog named Bobo and the dream he has.

POSTREADING DISCUSSION:

Ev Do you think Bobo's dream made him braver when he saw the big dog in real life. Why or why not? (Discuss.)

JOURNAL WRITING:

Ap/An **Group Activity -** "Chaining" - What happened in the story? (Children relate main events of story. Teacher draws/writes them in links of a chain.)

Example:

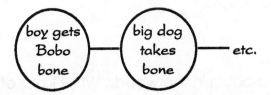

Ap/An **Prewriters -** Draw first and last parts of the story. (Or each child chooses a portion of the chain to illustrate and copies the appropriate sentences from the board. The sentences can be compiled into class books.)

Ap/An **Beginning Writers -** Draw and write three main things that happened in the story.

Sy **Experienced Writers -** Write what happened in the story in your own chain. Illustrate it.

Martha Alexander

BOBO'S DREAM

Draw the beginning, middle, and end of a dream you've had.

© 1991 by Incentive Publications, Inc., Nashville, TN.

Name _____

Martha Alexander

BOBO'S DREAM

How would the story have been different if Bobo were a big dog?

First, _____

_____

_____ .

Then, _____

_____

_____ .

Last, _____

_____

_____ .

Name _____

BOBO'S DREAM

MATH

BIG/LITTLE:
Categorize characters in the story as big and little. Use other things around the room for categorizing, such as objects or pictures of objects.

SCIENCE

HELPING EACH OTHER:
Learn how animals and people help each other.

SOCIAL STUDIES

SIMILARITIES/DIFFERENCES:
Discuss how Bobo's dream was the same as and different from the real-life story of the boy helping him with the bone.

FINE ARTS

COTTON DREAMING PICTURES:
Illustrate a dream you've had and surround it with pasted cotton balls.

LANGUAGE ARTS

TELL/ACT A DREAM:
In small groups, tell about or act out dreams you've had.

POBO'S DREAM

BIG/LITTLE:
Categorize characters in the story as big and little. Use other things around the room for categorizing, e.g. sort... a table or pictures of objects.

HELPING EACH OTHER:
Learn how animals and people help each other.

SIMILARITIES/DIFFERENCES:
Discuss how Pobo's dream was the same as and different from the real life story of the boy helping him with the bone.

COTTON DREAM PICTURES:
Illustrate a dream you've had and surround it with pasted cotton balls.

RE-ENACT A DREAM:
In small groups, tell about or act out dreams you've had.

Picture Books

WHISTLE FOR WILLIE

PREREADING DISCUSSION:

Ap Can you whistle? Was it hard to learn? How did you learn? Why did you want to whistle? (Discuss.)

This is a story about Peter, who wants to whistle for his dog Willie. See if he learns how.

POSTREADING DISCUSSION:

Ev How would the story be different if Peter didn't learn how to whistle? (Discuss.)

JOURNAL WRITING:

Ap **Group Activity -** Whom can you call if you whistle? What else can you do when you whistle? (Draw/list on board. Model writing sentences from information listed. Encourage children to be original in their own writing.)

Ap **Prewriters -** Draw the person or animal you would call if you whistled. Copy and complete the sentence, "I can call _____ ."

Ap **Beginning Writers -** Draw and write two things you could call if you whistled.

Sy **Experienced Writers -** Write at least three things you could call if you whistled. Illustrate your story when you have finished.

WHISTLE FOR WILLIE

Who is inside this carton?

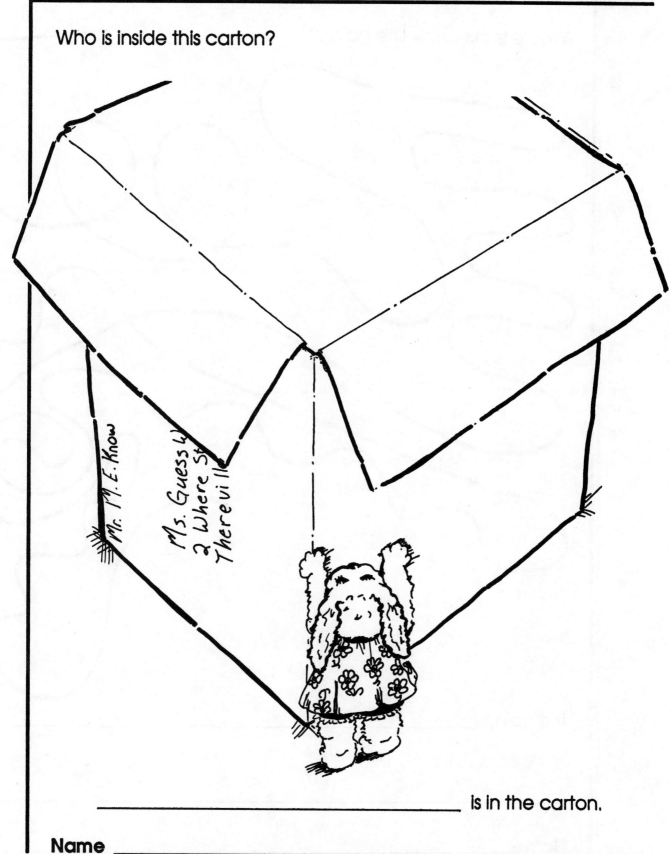

_____ is in the carton.

Name _____

WHISTLE FOR WILLIE

Sy
Beginning Writers

Where is this chalk line going?

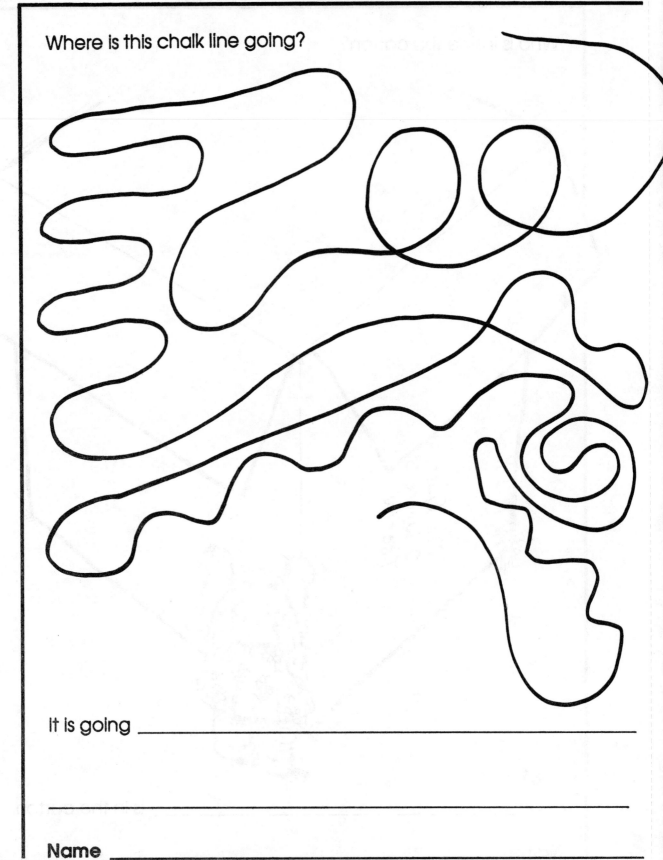

It is going _____

_____

Name _____

Ezra Jack Keats

WHISTLE FOR WILLIE

Who will wear this hat? What will he/she say?

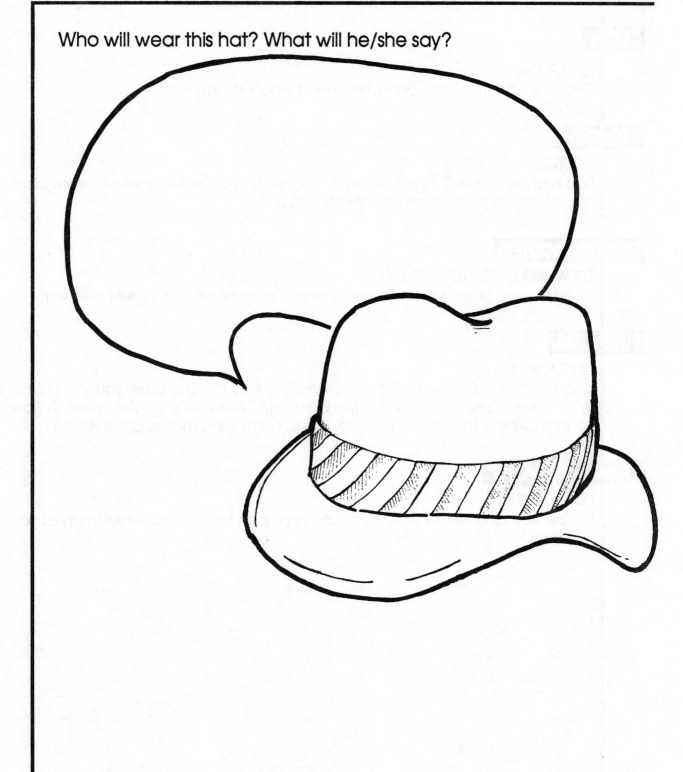

WHISTLE FOR WILLIE

MATH

GRAPHING:
Graph who in the class can whistle and who's still learning.

SCIENCE

SOUNDS:
Learn about other things that whistle (teapot, birds, whistles, etc.). Learn about the sounds other animals and things make.

SOCIAL STUDIES

TO WHISTLE/NOT TO WHISTLE:
Discuss good places to whistle and where one should not whistle and why.

FINE ARTS

SING/CHANT:
Sing songs and chants that involve whistling and making other sounds. ("Wheels on the Bus," "Let's Go Riding in the Car-Car," "BINGO," etc.) Also play "Follow the Leader" where the leader whistles, claps, hums, and makes other noises.

LANGUAGE ARTS

LISTEN, LISTEN:
Go outside and listen for all the sounds you can hear. Draw/write them as you are able.

GREEN EGGS AND HAM

PREREADING DISCUSSION:

Ev Do you think you would like green eggs and ham? Why or why not? (Discuss.)

This is a story about Sam-I-Am, who tries to serve green eggs and ham to his friend. Listen and see what happens.

POSTREADING DISCUSSION:

Ev How would the story end if the person did **not** like green eggs and ham? (Discuss.)

JOURNAL WRITING:

Ap **Group Activity** - Where are some places you might eat green eggs and ham? (Draw/list on board. Encourage rhyming words. Model writing sentences/rhyming passages from ideas generated.)

Ap **Prewriters** - Draw two places where you would eat green eggs and ham. (Encourage children to make the two places rhyme.)

Ap **Beginning Writers** - Draw and write two or three places where you would eat green eggs and ham.

Sy **Experienced Writers** - Write a poem about all the places you would eat green eggs and ham. Illustrate your poem.

GREEN EGGS AND HAM

Who will eat green eggs and ham?

Who will eat with Sam-I-Am?

_____ will eat green eggs and ham.

_____will eat with Sam-I-Am.

Name _____

GREEN EGGS AND HAM

Color the food items that would make up a nutritious breakfast.

Name _____

Dr. Seuss

GREEN EGGS AND HAM

Draw another cover for this book.

Name _____

GREEN EGGS AND HAM

MATH

MEASURING/COOKING:
Make green eggs and ham in the classroom. (Mix green food coloring in scrambled eggs while cooking them. Do the same with small pieces of ham.)

SCIENCE

GOOD MEAL:
Learn about what makes a good meal (something from each of the four food groups). Plan a good meal that includes green eggs and ham.

SOCIAL STUDIES

MAPPING:
Walk around the school looking for places (rhyming places if possible) where Sam-I-Am could serve green eggs and ham. Label the places on a map of the school.

FINE ARTS

WHERE, OH WHERE:
Draw some original places where green eggs and ham can be served.

LANGUAGE ARTS

POETRY:
Write a class poem about green eggs and ham.

BEST READING:
Divide into pairs or small groups. Take turns reading the story to one another. Once you feel you can do your best reading, tape-record yourself or read to someone from outside the classroom (principal, younger child, older student, custodian, secretary, etc.).

MILTON THE EARLY RISER

PREREADING DISCUSSION:

Ap Do you ever wake up before everyone else in your family? What do you do?

Milton wakes up early in this story. See what he does.

POSTREADING DISCUSSION:

Ev What do you think happened to Milton after the end of the story? Example:

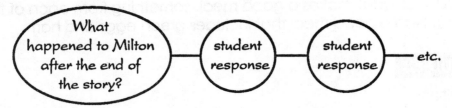

JOURNAL WRITING:

Ap **Group Activity** - Write a chart story from the postreading chaining activity.

Sy **Prewriters** - Illustrate a portion of the story and either copy the appropriate sentence from the story into your journal or attempt to write your own sentence.

Sy **Beginning Writers** - Draw and write what you think happened to Milton after the end of the story.

Sy **Experienced Writers** - Write what you think happened to Milton after the end of the story.

MILTON THE EARLY RISER

Everyone woke up.

Fold #1

I watched TV, played, and sang.

4.

3.

Fold # 2

1.

2.

Your name

the Early Riser

I got up ealry.
Everyone was asleep.

Robert Kraus

MILTON THE EARLY RISER

Whom would you wake up if you made noise in the morning?

I would wake up

I would wake up

I would wake up

I would wake up

Name

Robert Kraus

MILTON THE EARLY RISER

What do you do when you wake up early?

I _____
_____ .

I _____
_____ .

I _____

_____ .

Name _____

MILTON THE EARLY RISER

MATH

CLASSIFICATION:
Sort the types of animals in the story into categories.

GRAPHING:
Graph the number of each kind of animal in the book.

SCIENCE

COMPARE/CONTRAST:
Discuss how Milton used manners and was courteous; then talk about how he was rude.

SOCIAL STUDIES

HEALTH:
Learn the importance of getting enough sleep.

FINE ARTS

PAINTING:
Practice drawing and coloring pictures similar to the illustrations in the book.

PUPPETS:
Make puppets of Milton and other animals in the story.

LANGUAGE ARTS

PUPPET SHOW:
Put on puppet shows with the animal puppets made from the story.

FISH IS FISH

PREREADING DISCUSSION:

An How are a fish's world and a frog's world the same? How are they different? (Discuss.)

This story is about a little fish and a frog and the different worlds they live in.

POSTREADING DISCUSSION:

An How are a fish's world and a frog's world the same and different? (Draw/list on board.)

Same	Different
_____	_____
_____	_____
_____	_____

JOURNAL WRITING:

An **Group Activity** - What are some things you would tell the fish about your world? What are some things the fish would tell you about its world? (Draw/list on board. Encourage children to be original in their drawing/writing. Model writing sentences from information.)

Your World	Fish World
_____	_____
_____	_____
_____	_____

An **Prewriters** - Draw something you would tell the fish about your world. Then draw what the fish would tell you about its world. Copy and complete these sentences: "I will tell the fish about _____ . The fish will tell me about _____ ."

Ev **Beginning Writers** - Pretend you are the fish. Draw and list three things that make your world the best.

Sy/Ev **Experienced Writers** - The fish wants to know what makes your world so special. Write about one of your favorite things. Describe it well. Illustrate your work.

FISH IS FISH

Cut and paste the pictures in the right place.

--------------------------   --------------------------
water   ### land
--------------------------   --------------------------

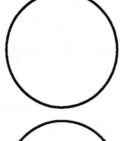 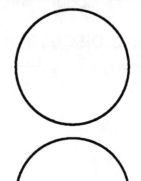

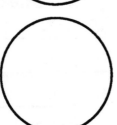 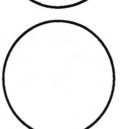

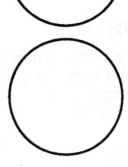

Name _____

FISH IS FISH

Fold # 1

The frog pushed him back in the water. "Fish is fish," the fish said. "The water is best for me."

The fish wanted to see the world. He flopped on the land but could not breathe.

4.   3.

Fold # 2

1.   2.

by _____

Fish is Fish

_____

A fish knew a frog. The frog told him about the world.

FISH IS FISH

Describe an animal. Draw what the fish thinks it looks like.

_____

(animal)

_____

_____

_____

_____

FISH IS FISH

MATH

CATEGORIZING:
On cards draw things that live on land and the water. In small groups categorize your pictures in as many different ways as you can.

SCIENCE

FISH AND FROGS:
Learn about the life cycles of fish and frogs. Compare and contrast them.

POND LIFE:
Study pond life.

SOCIAL STUDIES

I LIKE ME:
Just as the fish could live in the water and not on land, discuss things you can and can't do. Then just like the fish learned to love his world best, discuss what you like about yourself and your life.

FINE ARTS

FISHY PICTURES:
Draw what the fish might think some other animals look like (horses, turtles, pigs, elephants, etc.).

WATERCOLOR WASH:
Draw pictures of underwater life in crayon; then paint over it all with watercolor to simulate water.

LANGUAGE ARTS

DARING DESCRIPTIONS:
In pairs describe animals and other things.

THE THIRD STORY CAT

PREREADING DISCUSSION:

 If you stayed in the house all day, where would you want to go if you got out? (Discuss.)

This is the story of a cat named Alice, who lives on the third story of an apartment building. Listen to where she goes and what she does.

POSTREADING DISCUSSION:

 Do you think Alice will go back to the park again? Why or why not? Do you think Annie will leave the kitchen window open again? Why or why not? (Discuss.)

JOURNAL WRITING:

 Group Activity - Pretend you are Alice. How would you describe your day? (Draw/list responses on board. Model writing sentences from responses. Have children expand them with vivid, descriptive words.)

Where else would you want to go if you were Alice? Write about it. (Encourage children to use vivid, descriptive words in their writing.)

Prewriters - Draw one or two things you would do if you were Alice. Copy and complete this sentence from the board, "If I were Alice I would _____."

Beginning Writers - Draw and write about where you would go if you were Alice.

Experienced Writers - Write a story about where you would go if you were Alice. Illustrate it.

Leslie Baker

THE THIRD STORY CAT

If you were Annie, where would you let your cat go?

I would let my cat go _____ :

Name _____

Leslie Baker

THE THIRD STORY CAT

Follow the directions and draw where Alice went on the map of the park.

1. Draw a line from the apartment to the bird across the street.

2. Draw a line from the bird to the wall.

3. Alice jumps down from the wall and goes up a tree.

4. She rolls in the flower bed.

5. She fishes in the pond.

6. She sits under a bench.

Name _____

Leslie Baker

THE THIRD STORY CAT

Draw and describe where you would search for your cat if it were gone.

I would search _____.

I would search _____.

I would search _____.

Name _____

THE THIRD STORY CAT

MATH

GRAPH:
Help your teacher graph the kinds of pets you have or would like to have.

SCIENCE

CATS:
Learn about cats and the things they like to do.

SOCIAL STUDIES

PETS:
Discuss the responsibilities of having a pet, such as caring for it.

FINE ARTS

WATERCOLOR:
Study the watercolor illustrations in the book. Paint your own picture of the story.

LANGUAGE ARTS

OVER, UNDER, AROUND AND AROUND:
In small groups, write directions on cards. (Examples: over the table, under the chair, through the sandbox, on top of the bench.) One child from the group chooses a few cards and follows the directions as the rest of the group follows behind.

POINT OF VIEW:
In small groups, retell the story from Annie's point of view.

THERE'S A NIGHTMARE IN MY CLOSET

PREREADING DISCUSSION:

Ap Have you ever thought there was something scary in your room at night? What was it? (Discuss.)

Now this story is about a boy whose nightmare lived in his closet. Listen to what he does about it.

POSTREADING DISCUSSION:

Ev What do you think will happen if the second nightmare comes and sleeps with the boy? (Discuss.)

JOURNAL WRITING:

K **Group Activity** - Look at the picture of the nightmare from the book. Describe it. Expand your phrase with more descriptive words. (List descriptive phrases. Model writing full sentences from them.)

Sy **Prewriters** - Draw your own nightmare. Copy and complete the sentence, "My nightmare is _____."

Sy **Beginning Writers** - Draw and describe your nightmare.

Sy **Experienced Writers** - Describe your nightmare in detail. Draw it.

THERE'S A NIGHTMARE IN MY CLOSET

What's in this closet?

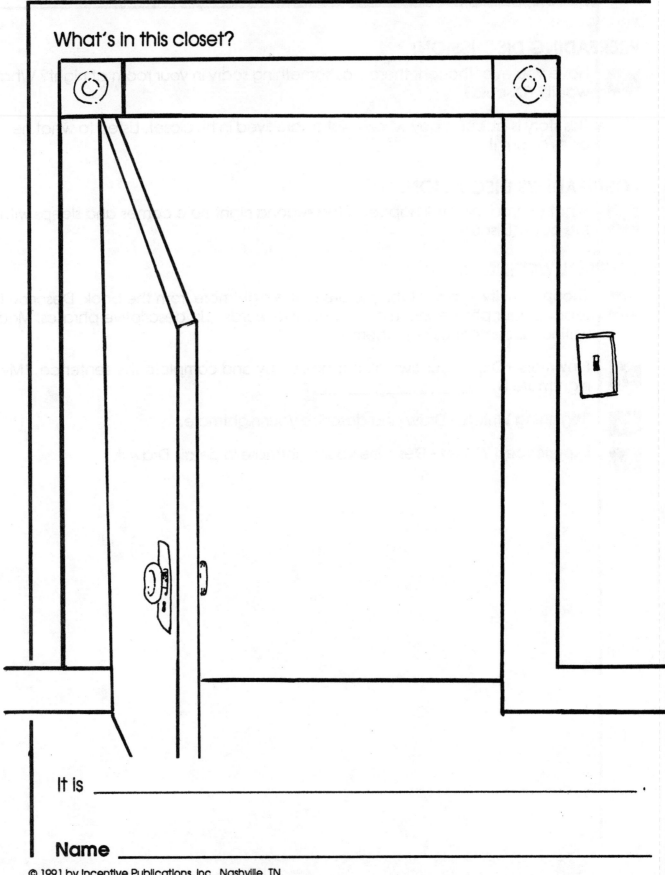

It is _____ .

Name _____

Mercer Mayer

THERE'S A NIGHTMARE IN MY CLOSET

Where does your nightmare live? What does it do?

My nightmare lives in my _____

_____.

It _____

_____.

Name _____

THERE'S A NIGHTMARE IN MY CLOSET

Experienced Writers

How would you catch your nightmare?

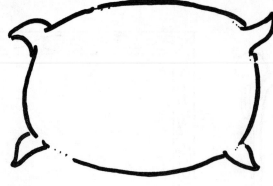

First I'd _____

_____

_____ .

Then I'd _____

_____

_____ .

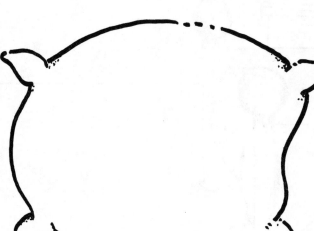

Last I'd _____

_____

_____ .

Name _____

THERE'S A NIGHTMARE IN MY CLOSET

MATH

GRAPHING:
Help your teacher graph bedtimes of children in your class, how many use a nightlight, how many share a bedroom, etc.

SCIENCE

SLEEP:
All animals need sleep. Learn about how much sleep children need. Recommend a good bedtime. Discuss bedtime routines. Suggest children spend half an hour in bed reading without TV before going to sleep. (It's a great way to wind down.)

SOCIAL STUDIES

BEING AFRAID:
Discuss things that scare children and how it's OK to be afraid. Then talk about what you can do about being afraid.

FINE ARTS

THREE-PART NIGHTMARES:
Fold paper into thirds accordion-style. With only the top third showing, draw the head of your nightmare and pass it to another child. That child will see only the second third and will draw the body and pass it to the next child. Without seeing the rest of it, the last child will draw the feet. When it's opened, a crazy nightmare will appear.

LANGUAGE ARTS

LISTEN, LISTEN, DRAW, AND WRITE:
As your teacher describes funny parts of a nightmare (three red noses, two little heads, one great foot, etc.), draw it. (Teacher gradually adds more detailed descriptions (two large purple ears, etc.)). After you have drawn the nightmare, either describe it to one another or write about it using the descriptive words.

ONE FINE DAY

PREREADING DISCUSSION:

 What would you do if you got really thirsty? Would it matter where you got something to drink? Even if it belonged to someone else? (Discuss.)

This is the story of a fox who was very thirsty. Listen to what happens when he gets something to drink.

POSTREADING DISCUSSION:

Do you think the fox was right to drink all the milk? Why or why not? How else could he have obtained a drink?

JOURNAL WRITING:

Ev **Group Activity** - How would the story be different if the fox hadn't drunk all the milk? (Draw/write responses.)

Example:

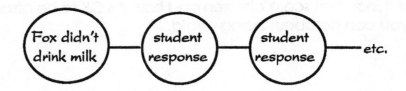

(NOTE: More than one chain can be generated, and ideas can chain out in more than one direction.)

C/Sy **Prewriters** - Choose one section of the chain to illustrate. Think of your own original ideas. Copy the appropriate sentence from the chain, or write your own.

Sy **Beginning Writers** - Draw and write your own three link chain of what would have happened if the fox hadn't drunk the milk.

Sy **Experienced Writers** - Write your own chain of what would have happened if the fox hadn't drunk all the milk. Illustrate it.

ONE FINE DAY

Sy
Prewriters

Cut out the fox puppet. Staple it together leaving a hole at the bottom so that is may be stuffed with the rest of this crumpled paper. Then, staple the hole.

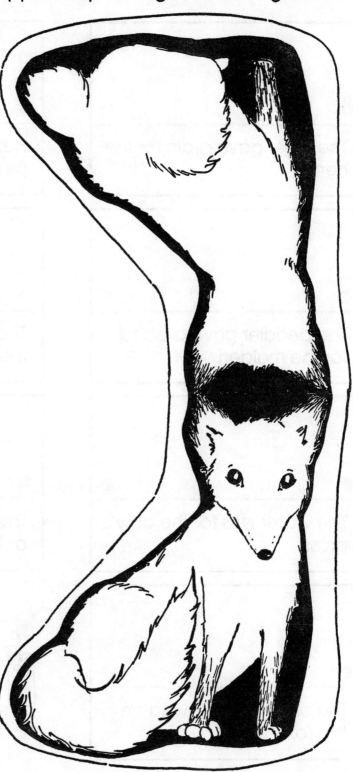

Name _____

ONE FINE DAY

Draw each picture. Then cut them out and string them together.

The Miller gave grain for the hen.

Hen gave an egg for the peddler.

The peddler gave a bead for the maiden.

The maiden gave a jug for the water.

The water was for the cow's grass.

The cow gave milk for the old woman.

The old woman sewed on the fox's tail.

© 1991 by Incentive Publications, Inc., Nashville, TN.

Name _____

ONE FINE DAY

What would the fox ask from you? What would you tell him to get?

ONE FINE DAY

MATH

COUNT 'EM UP:
Count how many things the fox had to do. How many animals, how many people?

CATEGORIZE:
Draw all the things from the story on cards. In small groups categorize them in as many ways as possible.

SCIENCE

FOXES:
Learn about foxes.

SOCIAL STUDIES

HELPING HANDS:
Discuss how people help each other by exchanging things for services.

FINE ARTS

SEWING:
Sew sock puppets of the fox (making sure to sew the tail on tight).

PAINTING:
Paint different scenes from the story.

LANGUAGE ARTS

PUPPET SHOW:
Retell the story with puppets.

CHAIN STORIES:
Act out "chain" stories from your journals.

NANA UPSTAIRS & NANA DOWNSTAIRS

PREREADING DISCUSSION:

Ap Think of a special older person in your life. What are some special things you do with him/her? What special name do you call him/her? (Discuss.)

This is a story about Tommy, who has two special older people in his life. He calls them Nana Upstairs and Nana Downstairs. Listen to what happens.

POSTREADING DISCUSSION:

Ap What are some of the special things you will remember about the old person in your life even after he/she has died?

JOURNAL WRITING:

An **Group Activity** - Discuss the happy and sad parts of the story. (List them on the board. Write a chart story summarizing the happy and sad parts dictated by the children.)

An **Prewriters** - Draw a happy and a sad part of the story. Copy and complete these sentences: "It was happy when _____ . It was sad when _____ ."

An **Beginning Writers** - Draw and write about a happy and a sad part of the story.

An **Experienced Writers** - Write about a happy and a sad part of the story.

NANA UPSTAIRS & NANA DOWNSTAIRS

Then Nana Downstairs died. A star was
in the sky. Now both Nanas are upstairs.

Fold # 1

One day Nana Upstairs died.
It was sad.

4.   3.

Fold # 2

1.   2.

by
_____

**Nana Upstairs &
Nana Downstairs**

One Nana lived upstairs.
One Nana lived downstairs.

Tomie de Paola

NANA UPSTAIRS & NANA DOWNSTAIRS

Who lives upstairs? Who lives downstairs?

Upstairs lives _____

Downstairs lives _____ .

Name _____

NANA UPSTAIRS & NANA DOWNSTAIRS

Look out your window. What do you see? What does it mean?

I see _____ .

It means _____

_____ .

Name _____

NANA UPSTAIRS & NANA DOWNSTAIRS

MATH

ESTIMATE:
In small groups, children estimate the number of candies in a package of candy mints. If mints are different sizes/shapes, categorize them. Your teacher will graph the results before you divide and eat them.

SCIENCE

STARS:
Learn about stars and falling stars. Discuss the myths and legends surrounding them.

SOCIAL STUDIES

ADOPT A GRANDPARENT:
Visit a rest home and "adopt" grandparents. Periodically write to them and visit them.

DEATH AND DYING:
Discuss feelings surrounding death of pets, grandparents.

FINE ARTS

SPECIAL TIMES DRAWINGS:
Draw/paint special events you remember having with older people.

LANGUAGE ARTS

INTERVIEWS:
Interview older people (even people at school — teachers, custodians, cafeteria workers) and write or tell about them. Find out things older people liked to do when they were young – favorite games, foods, etc.

CHAIN STORIES:
Act out "chain" stories from your journals.

TOO MANY BOOKS!

PREREADING DISCUSSION:

 What would it be like to have too many books? What would you do with them? How could you get rid of them? (Discuss.)

This story is about Maralou, who has too many books. See what she does with them.

POSTREADING DISCUSSION:

 Do you think Maralou will ever have too many books again? Why or why not? (Discuss.)

JOURNAL WRITING:

 Group Activity - Who are some people to whom you could give books? Where are some places you could give your books away? (Draw/list on board; then model writing sentences using the information.)

 Prewriters - Draw a picture of the person to whom you would give a book. Draw where you would take your book to give it away. Copy and complete this sentence, "I will give it to _____."

 Beginning Writers - Draw and write about two people to whom you would give books. Draw and write about two places you would take your books to give them away.

Experienced Writers - Write about the people to whom you would give your books and where you would take them to give them away. Tell why. Illustrate your story.

Caroline Feller Bauer

TOO MANY BOOKS!

Where are these books in your house?

The books are in my _____.

Name _____

Caroline Feller Bauer

TOO MANY BOOKS!

Draw the cover of a book you would like to have.

Name _____

TOO MANY BOOKS!

How could you earn money to buy books?

I could _____

_____

_____.

I could _____

_____

_____.

I could _____

_____

_____.

Name _____

TOO MANY BOOKS!

MATH

NUMBERS OF BOOKS/PAGES:
Keep track of the numbers of books and pages you read. Periodically combine the totals in your class to see how many books the class is reading as a whole. (For older children, you can even calculate the numbers of words.)

SCIENCE

READ ABOUT IT:
Discuss science topics of interest to the class and choose books with science themes during library time.

SOCIAL STUDIES

MY FAVORITE BOOKS:
Compile a list of 2 to 5 of your favorite books. In small groups explain why you like them.

FINE ARTS

POSTERS:
Make posters advertising favorite books and place them around the room, school, community.

LANGUAGE ARTS

SHARED READING:
In pairs or small groups, read your favorite books to one another.

TAPE-RECORD:
Practice reading a favorite book until you can read it to the very best of your ability. Then tape-record your reading. Others can listen to it at the listening post while following along with the book.

A HOUSE IS A HOUSE FOR ME

PREREADING DISCUSSION:

C What are some different kinds of houses for animals, people — anything you can think of? (List on board.)

This book is a poem about houses. Listen for all the different kinds of houses so you can add to the list.

POSTREADING DISCUSSION:

C What other kinds of houses were in the story? (Add to list on board.)

JOURNAL WRITING:

Ap **Group Activity** - Continue describing houses for animals, things, and people. Encourage rhyming words. (Draw and write them. Then model writing them into sentences.)

Ap **Prewriters** - Draw a house you would like to live in. Draw a house for something else. Copy sentences from the board:

"A _____ is a house for _____ ."

"A _____ is a house for _____ ."

Ap **Beginning Writers** - Draw and write about three different houses.

Sy **Experienced Writers** - Write a poem about houses. Illustrate it.

Mary Ann Hoberman

A HOUSE IS A HOUSE FOR ME

Draw who lives in each house. Cut and paste the drawings in the right place.

People   Others

tent   egg   flowerpot

igloo   house   bag

Name _____

Mary Ann Hoberman

A HOUSE IS A HOUSE FOR ME

Whose house is this?

I am a house for

_____ .

I am a house for

_____ .

A _____ Is a house for me!

A _____ is my house.

Make up your own.

A _____ is a house for _____ .

Name _____

Mary Ann Hoberman

A HOUSE IS A HOUSE FOR ME

Turn these shapes into houses. Draw and write whose houses
they are.

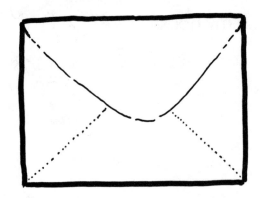

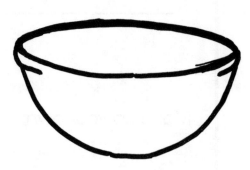

Name _____

A HOUSE IS A HOUSE FOR ME

MATH

CATEGORIZE:
Draw as many houses as you can think of on cards. In small groups, categorize them in as many ways as possible.

SCIENCE

ANIMAL HOUSES:
Learn about the different kinds of houses animals have.

SOCIAL STUDIES

SIMILARITIES/DIFFERENCES:
Discuss similarities and differences between houses for people and houses for animals.

FINE ARTS

COLLAGE:
Cut out magazine pictures and make a collage of different kinds of houses.

DREAM HOUSE DIORAMA:
Construct dioramas of a child's dream playhouse.

LANGUAGE ARTS

POETRY:
Write poems about houses and who/what lives in them.

THE PAPER CRANE

PREREADING DISCUSSION:

 How do you think a paper crane could help you if you were having trouble? (Discuss.)

This story is about how a paper crane helped a man who owned a restaurant.

POSTREADING DISCUSSION:

 Why do you think the stranger came back to get the crane? What do you think he will do with it now? (Discuss.)

JOURNAL WRITING:

 Group Activity - Chaining - What do you think happened to the stranger and the crane after the end of the story? (Draw/write a chain of the students' responses. Model writing sentences from responses.)

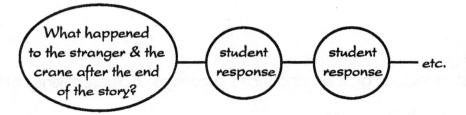

Prewriters - Draw one or two links from the chain and copy the appropriate sentence(s) from the board.

Beginning Writers - Draw and write your own three-link chain about what happened to the stranger and the crane after the story ended.

Experienced Writers - Write a complete chain story about the stranger and the crane after the book ended. Illustrate it.

THE PAPER CRANE

An
Prewriters

How would you pay for a meal if you didn't have money?

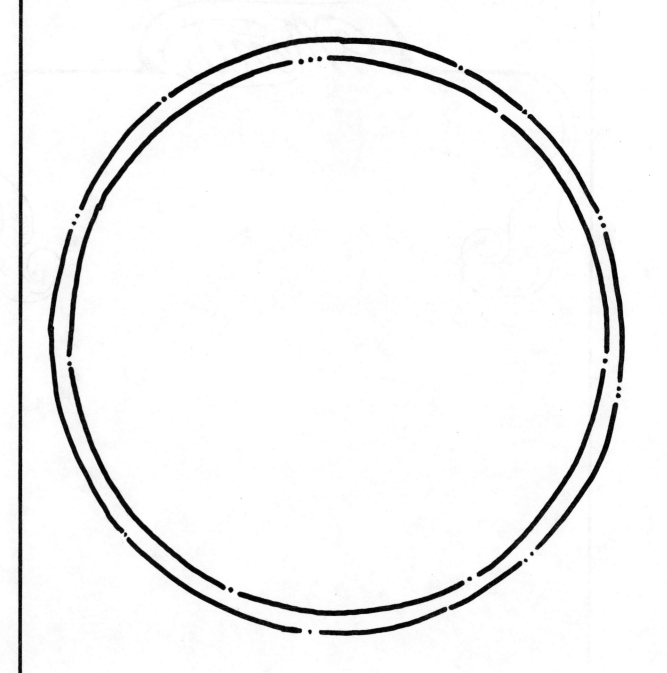

I would _____ .

Name _____

THE PAPER CRANE

Draw and write the foods you would make at your restaurant.

I would make _____

_____

Name _____

THE PAPER CRANE

Cut out the menu cover below. Make up a menu for your restaurant.

The Paper Crane Menu

THE PAPER CRANE

MATH

MEASURING/COOKING:
Cook recipes for things served in the restaurant.

SCIENCE

CRANES:
Learn about real cranes. Compare/contrast them to the paper crane.

SOCIAL STUDIES

RESPONSIBILITIES:
Discuss the responsibilities the boy had in the restaurant and how they were the same as and different from jobs you do at home.

MAPPING:
Study the highway blueprint in the book. Make maps of a road or highway and the stores and things that are beside it.

FINE ARTS

ORIGAMI:
Learn to make paper cranes and other origami shapes.

DANCE:
Practice dancing like the crane to music.

PAPER ILLUSTRATIONS:
Study the book's illustrations; then cut and paste paper to depict scenes from the book.

LANGUAGE ARTS

CLASS BOOK:
Compile, cut, and paste illustrations of scenes from the story into picture books. In small groups, take turns telling and retelling the story.

ONCE A MOUSE

PREREADING DISCUSSION:

Ap/Ev Is it better to be big or little? Why? Which would you rather be? Why? (Discuss.)

This story is about a hermit who helps a little mouse get bigger. See what happens.

POSTREADING DISCUSSION:

Ev Is being bigger better? Was it good for the tiger, or not? Why? (Discuss.)

JOURNAL WRITING:

Ev **Group Activity** - How would the story be different if the tiger had not thought of killing the hermit? (Chain the responses.)

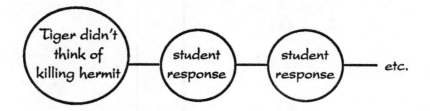

C/Sy **Prewriters** - Choose one section of the chain to illustrate (or think of your own). Copy the appropriate sentence from the board. Compile into class books.

Sy **Beginning Writers** - Draw and write your own chain about how the story would be different if the tiger had not thought of killing the hermit.

Sy **Experienced Writers** - Write your own story chain about what would happen if the tiger had not thought of killing the hermit. Illustrate it.

ONCE A MOUSE

An
Prewriters

What big animal do you want to be? What little animal do you want to be?

BIG

little

I want to be a big

I want to be a little

_____ .   _____ .

ONCE A MOUSE

Sy
Beginning Writers

Color the pictures. Cut them out and paste them on the map of the jungle.

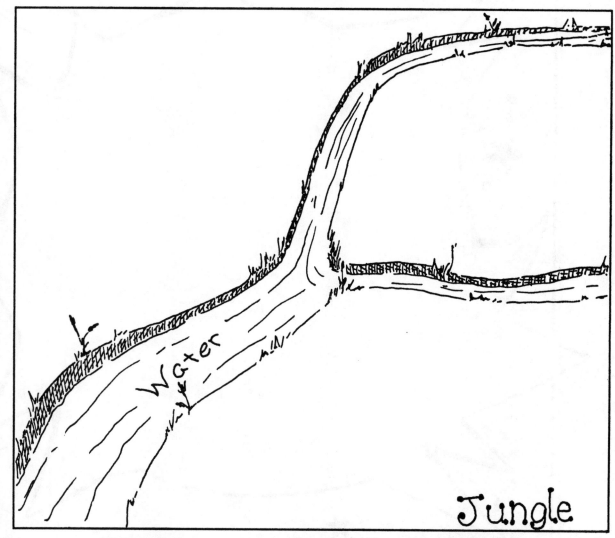

Name _____

Marcia Brown

ONCE A MOUSE

If you were the hermit, how would you use your magic on the tiger? Why?

I would use my magic to _____

_____

because _____

_____.

Name _____

ONCE A MOUSE

MATH

BIG/LITTLE:
Discuss relative sizes of a mouse to a cat and a dog to a tiger. Compare sizes of other things, too.

SCIENCE

JUNGLE:
Learn about jungle life.

SOCIAL STUDIES

BIG AND LITTLE:
Discuss the advantages and disadvantages of being big and the advantages and disadvantages of being little. In which situations is it best to be big? In which situations is it best to be little? Why?

FINE ARTS

PRINT MAKING:
Study the book's illustrations. Make prints from carved potatoes, onion halves, blocks of wood, and other things.

LANGUAGE ARTS

POINT OF VIEW:
In small groups, reenact the story, taking turns being the mouse, the tiger, and the hermit to understand each point of view.

THE PAPER BAG PRINCESS

PREREADING DISCUSSION:

 Should you choose your friends by the clothes they wear? Why or why not? (Discuss.)

This is the story of a beautiful princess who ends up wearing a paper bag. Listen to what happens.

POSTREADING DISCUSSION:

 Would you want a friend like Prince Ronald? Why or why not? Would you want a friend like Princess Elizabeth? Why or why not?

JOURNAL WRITING:

 Group Activity - What do you think happened to Princess Elizabeth after the end of the story? (Draw/list chain of events. Encourage children to be original with their own chains.)

Example:

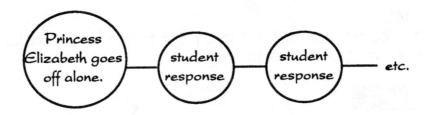

Prewriters - Draw two links of a chain. Copy and complete these sentences: "She _____ . Then she _____ ."

Beginning Writers - Draw and write a three-link chain.

Experienced Writers - Write a full chain of what happened to Princess Elizabeth after the end of the story. Illustrate it. (Another good chaining assignment would be to write a full chain of what happened to Prince Ronald.)

Robert N. Munsch

THE PAPER BAG PRINCESS

Color and cut out the princess and the dragon.

Paste them on paper bags.

Name _____

Robert N. Munsch

THE PAPER BAG PRINCESS

The dragon in this story can fly around the world.

Draw what your dragon can do.

My dragon can _____

_____.

Name _____

THE PAPER BAG PRINCESS

Sy
Experienced Writers

Prince Ronald needs to find a new wife. Make up a poster to be put all over his kingdom.

Name _____

THE PAPER BAG PRINCESS

MATH

MEASUREMENT/TIME:
Determine how far you can run in 10 seconds. Determine how far you can run in 20 seconds. How long does it take you to run around the playground? How long does it take you to run to the fence and back?

SCIENCE

DRAGONS AND OTHER LIZARDS:
Study lizards, and make up information on dragons. Discuss their similarities and differences.

SOCIAL STUDIES

FRIENDSHIP:
Discuss what friendship is. How do you choose a friend? Imagine a friend's house has burned down with all his/her family's clothes inside — would you still be a friend? How would you help your friend?

FINE ARTS

PAPER BAG CLOTHES:
Make clothing out of paper bags. A large grocery bag makes a good vest.

1. Cut out head and armholes.
2. Cut line down the middle.
3. Turn bag inside out and decorate.

LANGUAGE ARTS

PUPPET SHOW:
Retell the story with paper bag puppets.

TALK LIKE RONALD:
Practice talking in a snobby tone like Ronald.

STEVIE

PREREADING DISCUSSION:

Ap/Ev | What do you think it would be like to have a younger person come and live with you? (Discuss.)

POSTREADING DISCUSSION:

An/Ev | What were some good things and bad things about having Stevie around? (Discuss.)

JOURNAL WRITING:

An/Ev | **Group Activity** - What are some other good and bad things about having a younger person come and live with you? (Draw/list on board. Model writing sentences from information.)

Good	Bad
_____	_____
_____	_____
_____	_____

Ap/Ev | **Prewriters** - Draw a good thing and a bad thing about having a younger person around. Copy and complete these sentences: "It is good when he/she _____ ." "It is bad when he/she _____ ."

Ap/Ev | **Beginning Writers** - Draw and write a good thing and a bad thing about having a younger person around.

Ap/Ev | **Experienced Writers** - Write about how it would be good and bad to have a younger person around. Illustrate your writing.

STEVIE

He would do things I didn't like.

Fold #1

I missed him when he went away.

3.

4.

Fold #2

2.

1.

Stevie came to live with me.

Stevie

by _____

John Steptoe

STEVIE

If Stevie came to live at your house, what rules would you make for him?

One rule would be _____

_____

_____

_____ .

Another rule would be _____

_____

_____

_____ .

Name _____

STEVIE

What would your friends say if you brought Stevie along to play?

STEVIE

MATH

GRAPHING:
Help your teacher graph how many children in your class have younger brothers and sisters.

MEASURING:
Measure out cereal and milk for a younger person and an older person. Write down the recipe.

SCIENCE

CORNFLAKE SCIENCE:
After measuring out cereal/milk from the math activity, do science experiments to gauge how long it takes different cereals to get soggy. Graph results.

SOCIAL STUDIES

CROSS-AGE EXPERIENCE:
Play pair games, read books together, etc. Discuss beforehand which games and activities are appropriate for younger children. Compare experiences afterward in small groups.

FINE ARTS

CHALK DRAWINGS:
Study illustrations in the book. Make chalk drawings on different kinds of paper (long roll of paper, onion skin, paper bags, construction paper, etc.).

LANGUAGE ARTS

WRITE ABOUT IT:
After doing the cross-age experience for social studies, write about your experience. Make your stories into books and illustrate them.

LETTER:
Write a letter to Stevie as if you were Bobby/Robert.

ALEXANDER, WHO USED TO BE RICH LAST SUNDAY

PREREADING DISCUSSION:

 What do you do with the money you get? Why?

This story is about Alexander, who used to have money not so long ago. See what happens to it.

POSTREADING DISCUSSION:

Ev What do you think will happen when Alexander gets money again? Why?

JOURNAL WRITING:

An **Group Activity** - What will you do with a dollar? How many will you save? Spend? What will you save for? What will you spend it on? (Draw/write responses. Then model writing sentences from the information.)

Ev **Prewriters** - Draw what you will do with your dollar. Copy and complete this sentence, "I will _____ my dollar."

Ev **Beginning Writers** - Draw and write two or three things you will do with your dollar.

Ev **Experienced Writers** - Write about all the things you will do with your dollar. Illustrate your writing.

ALEXANDER, WHO USED TO BE RICH LAST SUNDAY

Anthony told Alexander to use his money to buy a new face. If you were buying a new face, how would it look? Cut it out and wear it.

Name _____

Judith Viorst

ALEXANDER, WHO USED TO BE RICH LAST SUNDAY

If you were a grandparent, what presents would you bring each person in your family?

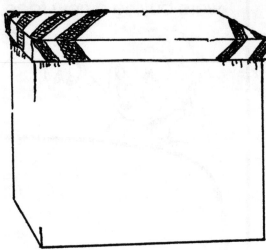

A _____

for _____ .

A _____

for _____ .

A _____

for _____ .

A _____

for _____ .

Name _____

Judith Viorst

ALEXANDER, WHO USED TO BE RICH LAST SUNDAY

What are you selling at your garage sale?

Make a poster detailing your items.

Garage Sale!

Name _____

ALEXANDER, WHO USED TO BE RICH LAST SUNDAY

MATH

ADD IT UP:
Add up how much Alexander's brothers have at the beginning of the book. Anthony had two dollars, three quarters, one dime, seven nickels, and eighteen pennies. Nicholas had one dollar, two quarters, five dimes, five nickels, and thirteen pennies. Total what Alexander spent his money on.

MONEY:
Learn the value of coins. Do money problems.

SCIENCE

RENT-A-PET:
Discuss pets you have and whether or not they would make good rentals, like the snake in the story.

SOCIAL STUDIES

MAPPING:
Map places around town Alexander could go with his bus tokens.

FINE ARTS

COLLAGE:
Make one collage of things you can get for free. Make another collage of things that cost money.

LANGUAGE ARTS

SHARING:
In small groups, share what you would do with your money. Also discuss the merits of saving and spending.

A NEW COAT FOR ANNA

PREREADING DISCUSSION:

An What steps do you think it takes to make a wool coat? (List on board.)

Example: wool from sheep

>   go to store

>   weave wool

>   buy thread

This is a story about the steps Anna and her mother go through to get a coat.

POSTREADING DISCUSSION:

C What were the steps Anna went through for her coat? (Circle correct responses and add as needed.)

Example: wool from sheep   spin into yarn

>   go to store   dye yarn

>   weave wool   cut the cloth

>   buy thread   sew it together

JOURNAL WRITING:

An **Group Activity -** Chain Activity: Chain the steps of Anna's coat in order. (Draw/write the steps. Model writing sentences from them.)

Example:

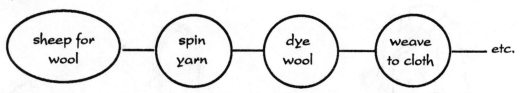

C **Prewriters -** Draw one or two steps of the chain and copy the appropriate sentence(s) from the board. These can be compiled into class books.

C **Beginning Writers -** Draw and write at least three steps in making the coat.

C **Experienced Writers -** Write about each step in making the coat. Illustrate your writing.

A NEW COAT FOR ANNA

Cut and paste these things in order.

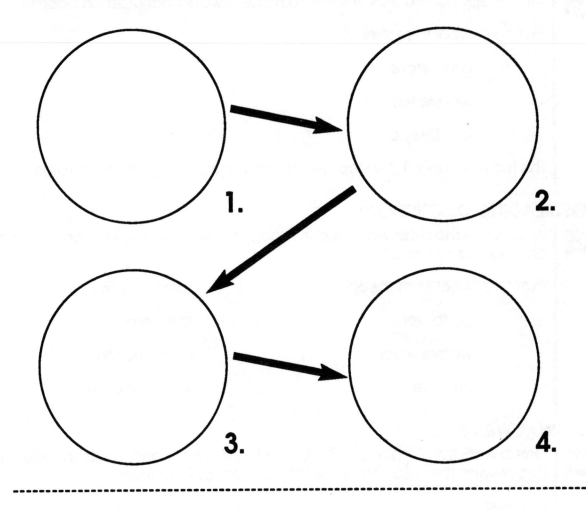

1.   2.

3.   4.

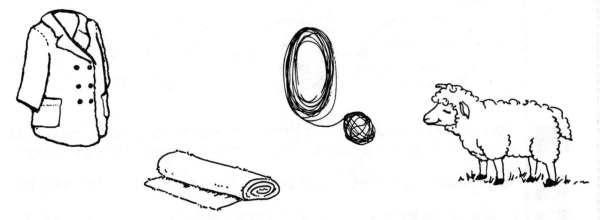

Name _____

Harriet Ziefert

A NEW COAT FOR ANNA

What are some things you would trade for a coat?

I would trade my _____

_____ .

I would trade my _____

_____ .

I would trade my _____

_____ .

Name _____

Harriet Ziefert

A NEW COAT FOR ANNA

If you were Anna, what presents would you give to each person who helped you?

sheep

farmer

old woman who spins

weaver

tailor

mother

Name _____

A NEW COAT FOR ANNA

MATH

MEASURING:
Measure each other like the tailor did for Anna's coat — shoulder to shoulder width, arm length, back of neck to back of knees.

SCIENCE

SHEEP:
Learn about sheep, how they use their wool, and how it is sheared and used by us.

SOCIAL STUDIES

WHERE OUR CLOTHES COME FROM:
Learn about the steps necessary to make other clothes you wear.
Example: cotton T-shirts, cotton plant, spinning, weaving, cutting, sewing.

FINE ARTS

SEWING:
Sew buttons on cloth and do other sewing activities to acquaint yourself with needle and thread (an important fine motor skill).

LANGUAGE ARTS

HOW TO:
In small groups, make large posters telling how to make a coat or T-shirt.

THE ISLAND OF THE SKOG

PREREADING DISCUSSION:

Ev What's the best way to meet someone new? (Discuss.)

This is the story of some mice who are about to meet a Skog. See how they go about it.

POSTREADING DISCUSSION:

Ev Do you think the mice were right or wrong to do what they did to meet the Skog? Why? Was there another way they could have met him? How?

JOURNAL WRITING:

Ev **Group Activity** - How would the story have been different if the mice brought the Skog a present instead of shouting at it? (Chain responses. Encourage children to be original when thinking of their own chains.)

Example:

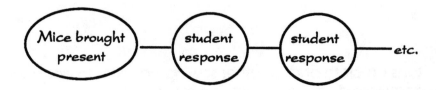

Ev **Prewriters** - Draw one or two sections of a chain. Copy and complete this sentence from the board, "The Skog would _____."

Ev **Beginning Writers** - Draw and write a three-link chain of what would happen if the mice brought the Skog a present instead of shouting at it.

Ev **Experienced Writers** - Write a complete chain of what would happen if the mice brought the Skog a present instead of shouting at it. Illustrate your chain.

Steven Kellogg

THE ISLAND OF THE SKOG

Draw your own Skog. Draw and write what you think it eats. Where do you think it sleeps? What makes it afraid?

It eats _____ .

It sleeps _____ .

It is afraid when _____ .

Name _____

Steven Kellogg

THE ISLAND OF THE SKOG

What would you take with you on a voyage?

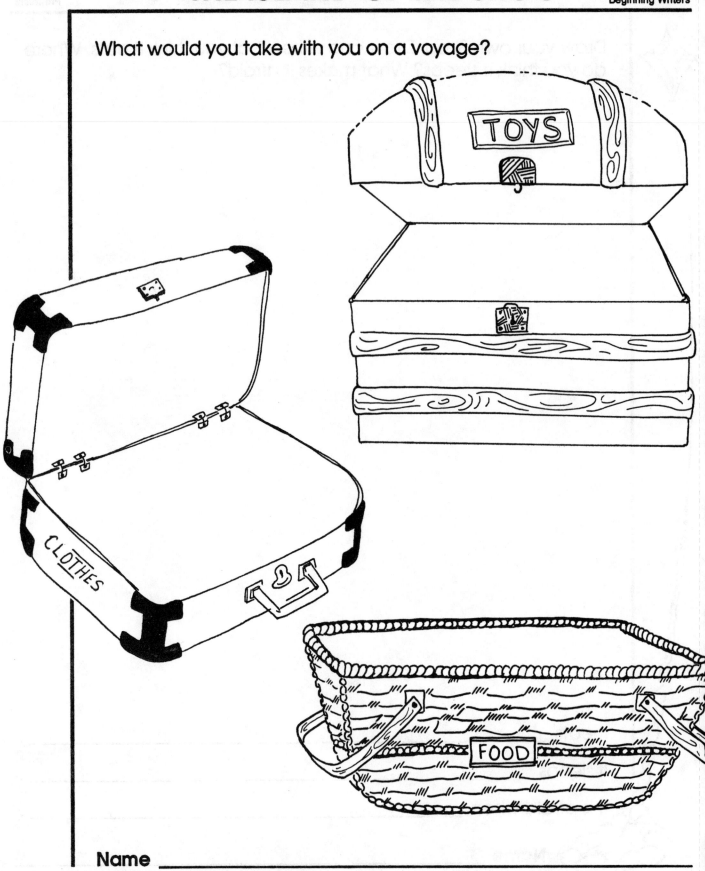

Name

THE ISLAND OF THE SKOG

Experienced Writers

Design your own island. Draw rivers, volcanoes, huts, trees, and other things you put in the key.

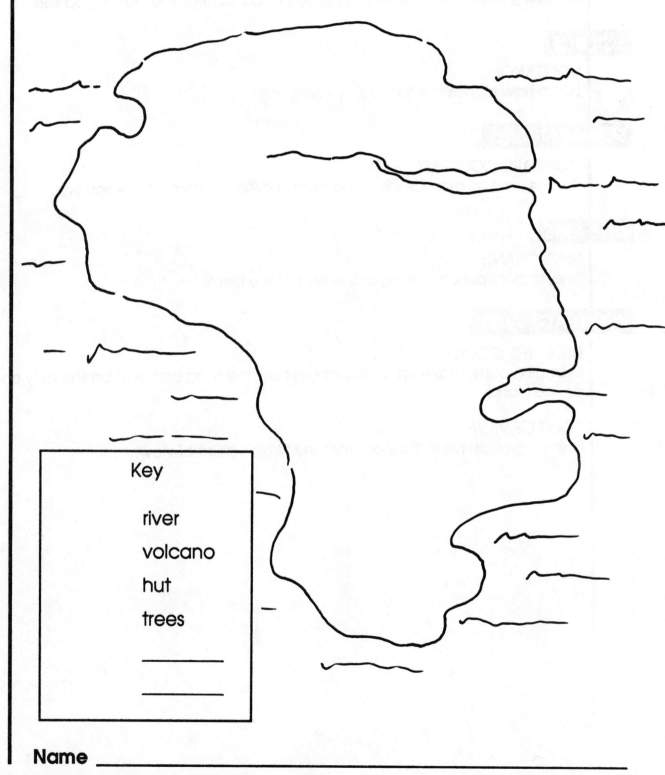

Key

river

volcano

hut

trees

_____

_____

Name _____

THE ISLAND OF THE SKOG

MATH

COUNT 'EM UP:
In small groups, look at a map or globe and count all the islands you see.

SCIENCE

VOLCANOES:
Learn how islands are formed by volcanoes.

SOCIAL STUDIES

COMPARE/CONTRAST:
Discuss how an island is the same as and different from where you live.

FINE ARTS

SING/CHANT:
Sing/chant Bouncer's song at the end of the book.

LANGUAGE ARTS

FILL IN THE STORY:
In small groups, make up a story about how the Skog came to be the only one on the island.

POINT OF VIEW:
In small groups, retell the story from the Skog's point of view.

EAST O' THE SUN & WEST O' THE MOON

PREREADING DISCUSSION:

Ev How important is it to make a promise? Why? (Discuss.)

This is the story of a maiden who makes a promise. See if she keeps it or not and what happens as a result.

POSTREADING DISCUSSION:

Ev How would the story have been different if the maiden had kept her promise? (Discuss.)

JOURNAL WRITING:

Ev **Group Activity** - If you were the frog prince, what three wishes would you ask for? (Draw/list on board, and model writing sentences from the information. Encourage children to be original with their own wishes.)

Sy **Prewriters** - Draw your three wishes. Copy and complete this sentence, "I would wish for _____."

Sy **Beginning Writers** - Draw and write your three wishes.

Sy **Experienced Writers** - Write what your three wishes would be. Illustrate them.

EAST O' THE SUN & WEST O' THE MOON

Draw your own troll. Tell about it.

My troll is _____.

Name _____

Mercer Mayer

EAST O' THE SUN & WEST O' THE MOON

Pretend you are riding the great fish. Where do you want to go?
Why?

I want to go _____

because _____

_____.

Name _____

EAST O' THE SUN & WEST O' THE MOON

Draw your own castle. Write about your kingdom.

My kingdom_____

_____

_____.

Name _____

EAST O' THE SUN & WEST O' THE MOON

MATH

HOW LONG/HOW FAR:
Calculate how long the maiden was gone and how far she had to travel.

SCIENCE

FROGS:
Learn about frogs. Compare and contrast them to the frog in the story.

SOCIAL STUDIES

KEEPING PROMISES:
Discuss keeping promises. What kind of promises should be kept, what kind of promises should be told, etc.

MAPPING:
Make up a map of where the maiden went throughout the story. Learn about directions — north, south, east, west.

FINE ARTS

MURAL:
Make a class mural depicting the journey the maiden took to the land east of the sun and west of the moon.

DIORAMA:
Construct dioramas from different parts of the story.

LANGUAGE ARTS

TELL A TALE:
In small groups, make up and write a story telling how the prince was turned into a frog by the trolls.

THE ELEPHANT'S CHILD

PREREADING DISCUSSION:

Ev | Is it good to be curious and ask questions? Why or why not? (Discuss.)

This is a famous story by a famous author. It is about a curious little elephant who asks many, many questions. Listen to what happens to him.

POSTREADING DISCUSSION:

Ev | How would the story have been different if the elephant's child wasn't so curious and didn't ask so many questions?

Example:

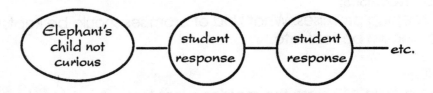

JOURNAL WRITING:

An | **Group Activity** - What are some other things you think the elephant's child couldn't do before but can do now with a long nose? (Discuss and list on the board. Model writing sentences from the lists. Encourage children to think of original ideas.)

Couldn't Do	Can Do
_____	_____
_____	_____
_____	_____

An | **Prewriters** - Draw one or two things the elephant's child couldn't do with his short nose but can do with his long one. Copy and complete this sentence, "He can _____ with his long nose."

An | **Beginning Writers** - Draw and write two or three things the elephant's child couldn't do before but can do now.

An | **Experienced Writers** - Write as many things as you can think of that the elephant's child couldn't do before but can do now with his long nose. Illustrate your writing.

THE ELEPHANT'S CHILD

Cut out the elephant's nose. Put it on your face with a string. Act out the story.

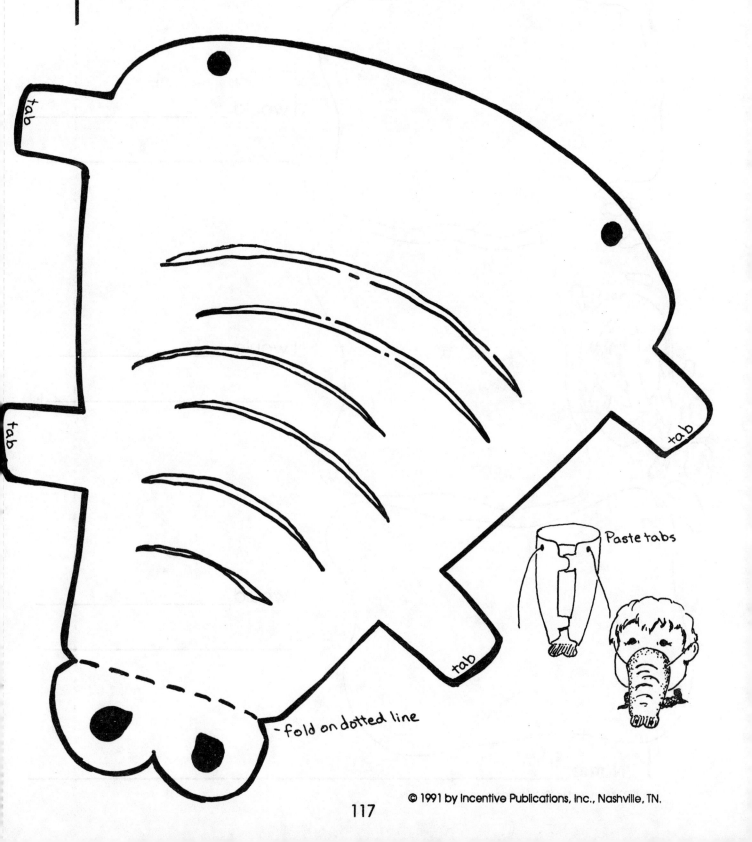

Paste tabs

fold on dotted line

Rudyard Kipling

THE ELEPHANT'S CHILD

What would you do with a long nose?

I would _____

_____ .

I would _____

_____ .

I would _____

_____ .

Name _____

THE ELEPHANT'S CHILD

When the elephant's child grows up, what will it say to a curious little elephant who asks questions?

Name _____

THE ELEPHANT'S CHILD

MATH

ESTIMATING:
In small groups, estimate the length of an elephant's trunk and draw it.

GRAPHING:
Graph elephant trunk estimates.

SCIENCE

ELEPHANTS & CROCODILES:
Study elephants and crocodiles. Compare and contrast them.

ENDANGERED SPECIES:
Learn about the conditions endangering the elephant.

SOCIAL STUDIES

MAPPING:
Learn about the jungles and rivers of Africa. Plot them on maps.

PUNISHMENT:
Discuss why the elephant's child was spanked. Did it help him or not? What would be another way of dealing with his questions?

FINE ARTS

CLAY ELEPHANTS:
Model elephants with short and long noses out of clay.

LANGUAGE ARTS

STORYTELLING:
In small groups, make up stories about how animals got specific attributes:
        Why cats have long tails,
        Why dogs bark,
        Why mice eat cheese,
        Why birds fly, etc.

THE GIRL WHO LOVED WILD HORSES

PREREADING DISCUSSION:

Have you ever loved or been close to an animal? What was it like? Could you talk with it? Could it talk to you? (Discuss.)

This is a Plains Indian legend about a girl who loved wild horses very, very much. Listen to what she does with them.

POSTREADING DISCUSSION:

How do you think the girl's family felt when she left to live with the horses? Why? What do you think would have happened if she had stayed with her people instead of going with the horses? Why?

JOURNAL WRITING:

Group Activity - Letter Writing. Using symbol language, write a group letter from the sick girl to her parents explaining why she must leave. Symbol Language:

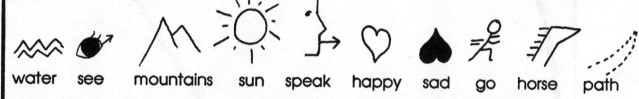

water   see   mountains   sun   speak   happy   sad   go   horse   path

For added interest, write on brown construction paper in the shape of an animal skin:

cut away

Prewriters - Using letter format, copy sentence(s) from the board, or write your own story using symbol language. Draw a picture to go with your writing.

Beginning Writers - Pretend you are the sick girl. Write a symbol language letter to your family telling why you have to go.

Experienced Writers - Pretend you are the sick girl. Write a symbol language letter to your family telling why you have to go.

THE GIRL WHO LOVED WILD HORSES

Decorate this tepee. Cut it out and paste it together.

← top →

Name _____

THE GIRL WHO LOVED WILD HORSES

Draw and write what presents you would give the horses. Draw the designs you would paint on them.

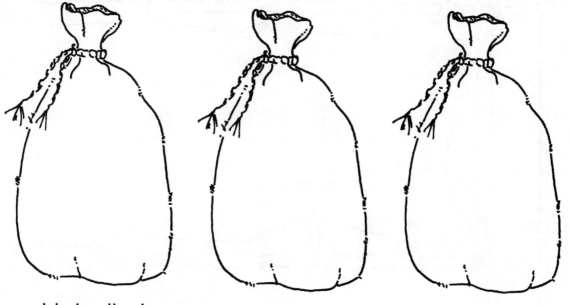

I would give the horses:

_____   _____   _____

Here are the designs I would paint on their bodies.

Name _____

Paul Goble

THE GIRL WHO LOVED WILD HORSES

What animals would you want to live with? Why?

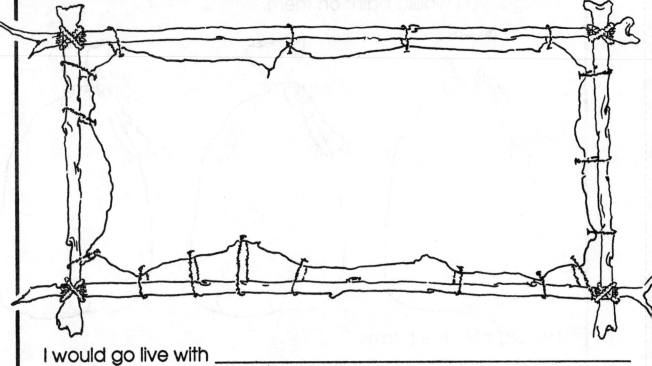

I would go live with _____

because _____ .

What presents would you bring your family every year?

Name _____

THE GIRL WHO LOVED WILD HORSES

MATH

MEASURING/COOKING:
Try this recipe.

BEEF JERKY

3 lbs. lean round steak cut into very thin slices ($1/4$ inch)
Marinade: $3/4$ cup soy sauce
2 tsp. garlic powder (or 4 cloves minced garlic)
1 tsp. pepper

1. Marinate beef strips for 6-8 hours
2. Spread beef strips on racks on cookie sheets in oven at low temperature (150° - 200°) for eight hours or overnight until moist-dry.

SCIENCE

PLAINS ECOSYSTEM:
Study the plants and animals of the plains.

SOCIAL STUDIES

PLAINS INDIANS:
Learn about the Plains Indians.

FINE ARTS

TEPEES:
Make tepees of straws, pins, clay, and paper. Set up an Indian camp.

WEAVING:
Weave paper place mats.

SING/CHANT:
Sing/chant the songs at the end of the book.

LANGUAGE ARTS

PLAY:
In small groups, act out the story, taking turns being the girl and members of the family to understand each point of view.

POEM/SONG:
Write other poems or songs the Indians may have sung or chanted.

MOLLY'S PILGRIM

PREREADING DISCUSSION:

 What is a pilgrim? Can people still be pilgrims today? Why or why not?

This is the story about Molly, a Jewish girl from Russia, and the pilgrim she is asked to make in her new school.

POSTREADING DISCUSSION:

 Do you think Elizabeth and her friends made fun of Molly after the story? Why or why not?

JOURNAL WRITING:

 Group Activity - Think about your family. What would your pilgrim look like? (Draw and list ideas on the board. Model writing sentences from children's listed ideas using descriptive words. Encourage children to be original in their own writing.)

 Prewriters - Draw what your pilgrim would look like. Copy and complete this sentence, "My pilgrim is _____ ."

 Beginning Writers - Draw and write what your pilgrim looks like.

 Experienced Writers - Write about your pilgrim - where is it from? What does it look like? Draw a picture of it.

MOLLY'S PILGRIM

Draw a picture of yourself. Then decorate the clothespin to look like you.

Name

Barbara Cohen

MOLLY'S PILGRIM

Who are the people in your family?

GRANDMOTHER

GRANDFATHER

GRANDMOTHER

GRANDFATHER

MOTHER

FATHER

ME

Name _____

MOLLY'S PILGRIM

What will Molly's mother and Miss Strickley, her teacher, talk about?

Name _____

MOLLY'S PILGRIM

MATH

MEASURING/COOKING:
Prepare food for a class Thanksgiving.

GRAPHING:
Help your teacher graph the cultural backgrounds of the children in your class (Scottish, Irish, African, Italian, Middle Eastern, Asian, Native American, etc.).

SCIENCE

HARVEST:
Learn about the harvest of food in your area. Learn about the planting and growing cycles of the plants. When and how are they planted? How are they harvested and readied for market?

SOCIAL STUDIES

FAMILY HISTORIES:
Interview your parents and learn about your family history. Write and tell about what you learn.

MAP:
Make a map of Plymouth, Massachusetts.

TABERNACLES:
Learn about the Jewish holiday of Tabernacles.

FINE ARTS

CLOTHESPIN DOLLS:
Make pilgrims from your family history.

PLYMOUTH VILLAGE:
Make a model of Plymouth Village.

LANGUAGE ARTS

FAMILY HISTORIES:
In small groups or individually, write or tell about your family history.

THANKFULNESS:
In small groups, discuss and record things for which you are thankful.

POINT OF VIEW:
Retell the story from Elizabeth's point of view.

Novels

THE ONE IN THE MIDDLE IS THE GREEN KANGAROO

CHAPTERS 1 and 2

PREREADING DISCUSSION:

Ap/Ay How many brothers and sisters do you have? How is this good? How is this bad? (Discuss.)

This is a story about Freddy, who is a middle child. See if his feelings are the same as yours.

POSTREADING DISCUSSION:

C/Ap What feelings did Freddy have about being in the middle? (List on the board.)

Good   Bad

_____   _____

JOURNAL WRITING:

Ap/Ev **Group Activity -** What are some good and bad things about being the child you are in your family? (Draw/list responses. Model writing sentences from information. Encourage children to think of original thoughts for their own writing.)

Good   Bad

_____   _____

_____   _____

_____   _____

 Prewriters - Draw a good thing and a bad thing about being the child you are in your family. Copy and complete these sentences: "It is good because _____ . It is bad because _____ ."

 Beginning Writers - Draw and write a good thing and a bad thing about being the child you are in your family.

Ap/Ev **Experienced Writers -** Write some good and bad things about your birth order in your family. Illustrate your writing.

THE ONE IN THE MIDDLE IS THE GREEN KANGAROO

Prewriters

Can you be a green kangaroo? Draw what you can do to be a green kangaroo.

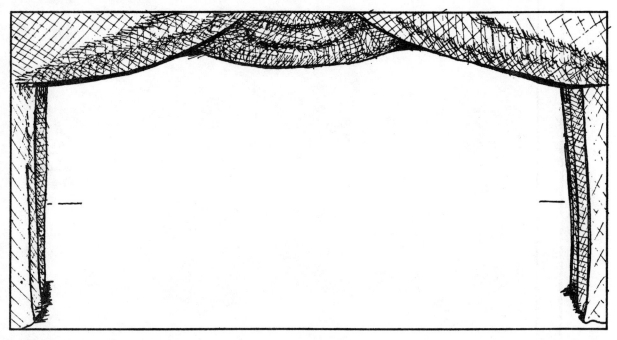

I can _____ .

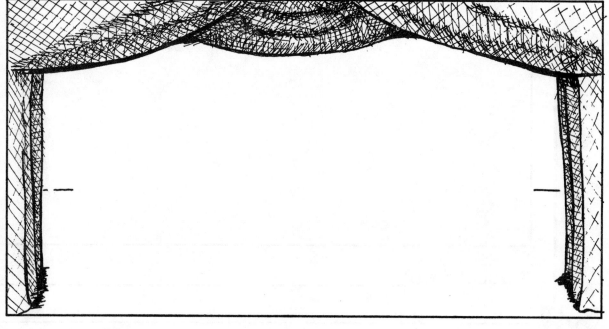

I can _____ .

Name _____

THE ONE IN THE MIDDLE IS THE GREEN KANGAROO

Draw what you think Freddy's room would look like if he had one.

It would have _____

_____.

Name _____

THE ONE IN THE MIDDLE IS THE GREEN KANGAROO

Pretend you will be in a play. Make a poster advertising it.

THE ONE IN THE MIDDLE IS THE GREEN KANGAROO

CHAPTERS 3 and 4

PREREADING DISCUSSION:

 How would you feel if you were going to be in a play in front of an audience? Why? (Discuss.)

Listen to how Freddy feels.

POSTREADING DISCUSSION:

 What kinds of things make you feel special? (Discuss.)

JOURNAL WRITING:

 Group Activity - What things do you do or have you done that make you feel special in your family? (List phrases on the board. Model writing sentences using listed phrases.)

 Prewriters - Draw something you do that makes you feel special. Copy and complete this sentence, "I feel special when I _____ ."

 Beginning Writers - Draw and write things you do that make you feel special.

 Experienced Writers - Write about a time you did something that made you feel special. Illustrate your story.

THE ONE IN THE MIDDLE IS THE GREEN KANGAROO

Draw your face on the puppet. Color it and cut it out. Do a puppet show.

Name

THE ONE IN THE MIDDLE IS THE GREEN KANGAROO

Here are the people in the play with you. Draw your friends and the parts they would play.

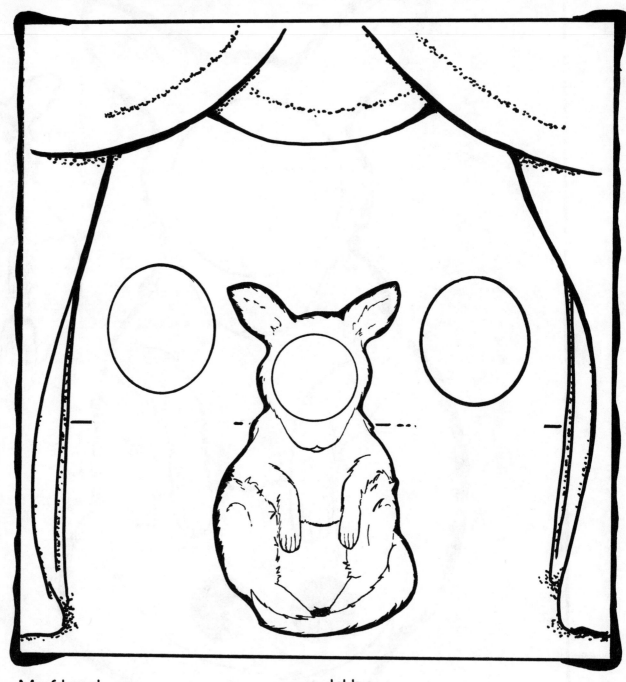

My friend _____ would be _____ .

My friend _____ would be _____ .

Name _____

THE ONE IN THE MIDDLE IS THE GREEN KANGAROO

What would you say if you were the green kangaroo?

Name _____

THE ONE IN THE MIDDLE IS THE GREEN KANGAROO

MATH

GRAPHING:
Where are you in the family? How many are middle children? Oldest? Youngest?

SCIENCE

COMPARE/CONTRAST KANGAROO:
Learn about real kangaroos. Then compare and contrast Freddy's green kangaroo with them.

SOCIAL STUDIES

I AM SPECIAL:
Discuss and record ways you are different and special.

SIMILARITIES/DIFFERENCES:
In small groups, discuss your own family relationships and how they are similar and different from Freddy's.

FINE ARTS

PUPPETS:
Make green kangaroo puppets.

DIORAMA:
Construct dioramas of major parts of the story.

LANGUAGE ARTS

PUPPET SHOW:
Put on a puppet show with green kangaroo puppets.

PLAY:
Make up and perform a class play with a green kangaroo in it.

THE STORIES JULIAN TELLS

THE PUDDING LIKE A NIGHT ON THE SEA

PREREADING DISCUSSION:

 What do you think lemon pudding would taste like? (Discuss. Encourage children to give colorful, vivid descriptions.)

This story is about lemon pudding that tasted like a night on the sea. Listen for other descriptions of it.

POSTREADING DISCUSSION:

 Do you think Julian and Huey really meant to eat all the pudding? Why or why not? (Discuss.)

JOURNAL WRITING:

 Group Activity - What are your favorite desserts? What do they taste like? (Draw and write on the board. Model writing sentences from student information. Encourage children to use descriptive words in their responses.)

 Prewriters - Draw your favorite dessert. Copy and complete these sentences: "My favorite dessert is _____ . It tastes like _____."

 Beginning Writers - Draw and write about your favorite desserts and what they taste like. Use descriptive words.

 Experienced Writers - Write a story about your favorite dessert and describe how it tastes.

THE STORIES JULIAN TELLS

Draw where your hiding place is in your house.

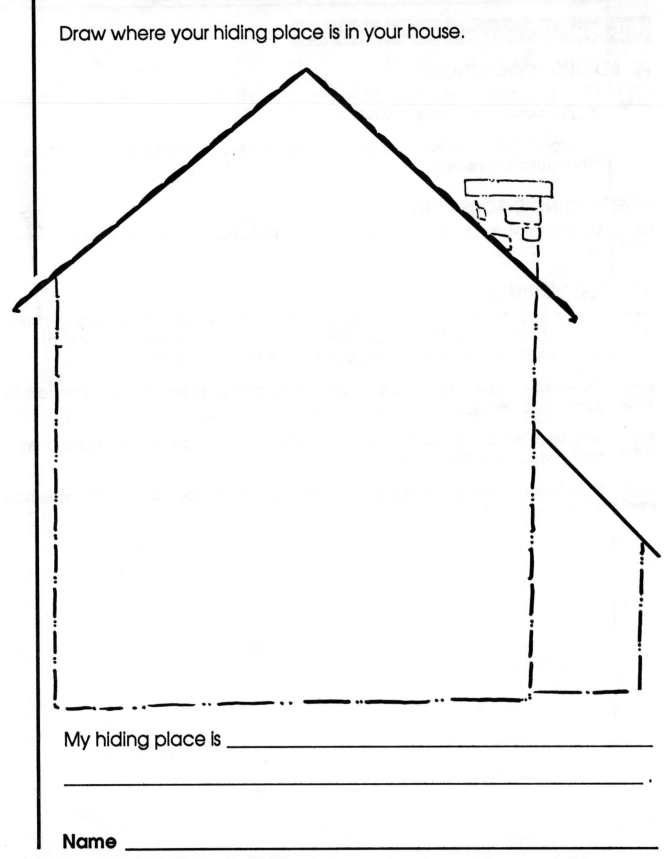

My hiding place is _____

_____.

Name _____

THE STORIES JULIAN TELLS

An
Beginning Writers

Draw the ingredients for your favorite dessert.

What are they?

_____   _____

_____   _____

_____   _____

Name _____

THE STORIES JULIAN TELLS

Sy
Experienced Writers

Make a poster advertising this story.

THE STORIES JULIAN TELLS

CATALOG CATS

PREREADING DISCUSSION:

Ap Have you ever told a fib? Did the person believe it? How did you feel about it? (Discuss.)

In this story Julian tells a fib about catalog cats. See what happens.

POSTREADING DISCUSSION:

Ev Do you think Julian's father got mad at him after the story was over? Why or why not? (Discuss.)

JOURNAL WRITING:

Sy **Group Activity -** What kind of catalog cats would you request? What would you want them to do? (Draw/write on board. Encourage descriptive phrases. Model writing and expanding sentences using vivid, descriptive words.)

Sy **Prewriters -** Draw the catalog cat you want. Copy and complete this sentence, "The catalog cat I want is _____ ."

Sy **Beginning Writers -** Draw and write about the catalog cats you want to order.

Sy **Experienced Writers -** Write a letter requesting the catalog cats you want. Draw them.

THE STORIES JULIAN TELLS

Ap/Sy
Prewriters

Draw what these catalog cats are doing.

This catalog cat is _____ .

This catalog cat is _____ .

Name _____

THE STORIES JULIAN TELLS

What are the catalog cats doing in your dream?

The cats are _____

_____

_____.

Name _____

THE STORIES JULIAN TELLS

Draw two catalog cats and write a description of them on this catalog page.

SPECIAL ON CATALOG CATS

Name _____

THE STORIES JULIAN TELLS

OUR GARDEN

PREREADING DISCUSSION:

C What steps do you go through to plant a garden? (Draw/list on board.)

Example: get seeds

                   put in ground

                   water

Listen to the steps Julian goes through to plant his garden.

POSTREADING DISCUSSION:

C What steps did Julian go through to plant his garden? (Circle and add steps as necessary.)

Example: get seeds   dig dirt

                   put in ground   pull weeds

                   water   make ground smooth

                                                watch them grow, etc.

JOURNAL WRITING:

C **Group Activity** - Julian and Huey got two special plants. What were they? How did they look? How did they taste? (Draw/write on board. Model writing sentences from information.)

Sy **Prewriters** - Draw your own special plant. Copy and complete these sentences: "My plant is a _____ . It tastes _____ .

Sy **Beginning Writers** - Draw and write about your own special plant.

Sy **Experienced Writers** - Write a story about your plant — what it looks like, and how it tastes.

THE STORIES JULIAN TELLS

Color and string together the steps Julian went through to grow his garden.

Got the seeds

Watered them

Put in ground

The plants grew

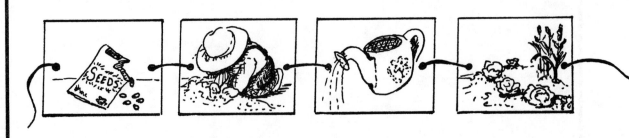

Name _____

THE STORIES JULIAN TELLS

Ap/Sy
Beginning Writers

What would it look like to have plants growing out of your hands and knees? Draw your ideas.

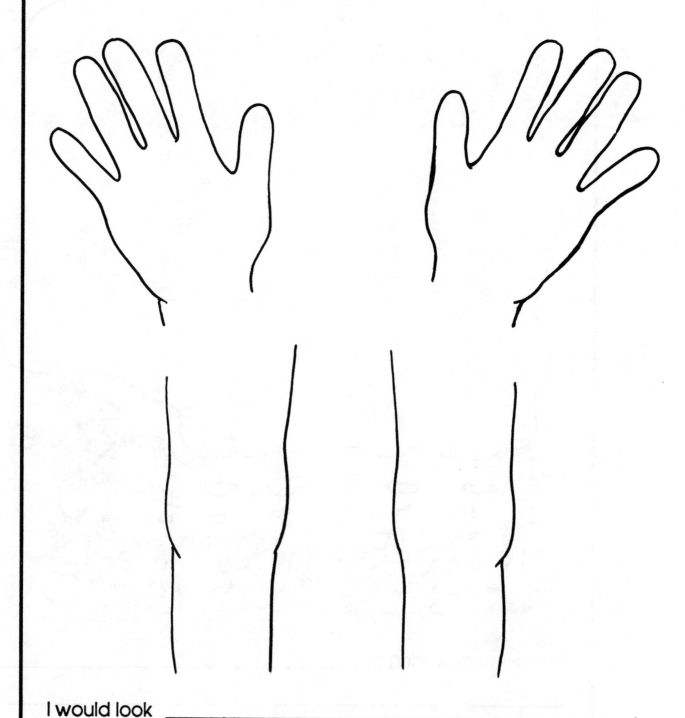

I would look _____ .

Name _____

THE STORIES JULIAN TELLS

Draw what you think the seeds were dreaming.

They were dreaming of _____

_____.

Name _____

THE STORIES JULIAN TELLS

BECAUSE OF FIGS

PREREADING DISCUSSION:

Ap What kinds of presents do you get for your birthday? Have you ever received a strange present? What was it? (Discuss.)

In this story Julian gets an unusual present for his birthday. See what it is and what he does with it.

POSTREADING DISCUSSION:

Ev Do you think Julian's father ever knew that Julian was eating the leaves? Why or why not? Do you think he would be mad about it? Why or why not?

JOURNAL WRITING:

Ev **Group Activity** - How would the story be different if Julian hadn't eaten the fig leaves? (Chain student responses.)

Example:

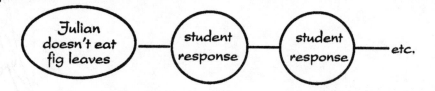

C/Sy **Prewriters** - Draw two links in the chain and copy the appropriate sentences, or draw two links of an original idea.

Sy **Beginning Writers** - Draw and write a three-link chain about what would happen.

Sy **Experienced Writers** - Write your own chain about what would happen. Illustrate it.

THE STORIES JULIAN TELLS

What do you eat to grow tall?

I eat _____

_____ to grow tall.

Name _____

THE STORIES JULIAN TELLS

What present would you give Julian? Why?

To: Julian
From:

I would give him _____

because _____

_____ ,

Name _____

THE STORIES JULIAN TELLS

What kind of tree would you want? Why?

I want a _____ tree

because _____

_____ .

Name _____

THE STORIES JULIAN TELLS

MY VERY STRANGE TEETH

PREREADING DISCUSSION:

Ap Have you ever had a loose tooth? What did it feel like? (Discuss.)

In this story Julian has a loose tooth. Listen to what happens.

POSTREADING DISCUSSION:

Ev What do you think will happen at school when Julian has no cave-boy teeth to show? Why? (Discuss.)

JOURNAL WRITING:

Ap **Group Activity** - What are some of the ways your teeth have come out? (Draw/list ideas on board; then write a chart story from the list.)

Ap **Prewriters** - Draw one way you lost a tooth. Copy and complete this sentence, "I lost my tooth when _____ ."

Ap **Beginning Writers** - Draw and write about the ways you've lost your teeth.

Ap **Experienced Writers** - Write a story about losing one of your teeth. Illustrate it.

THE STORIES JULIAN TELLS

Cut out the tooth puppet. Do a puppet show about losing a tooth.

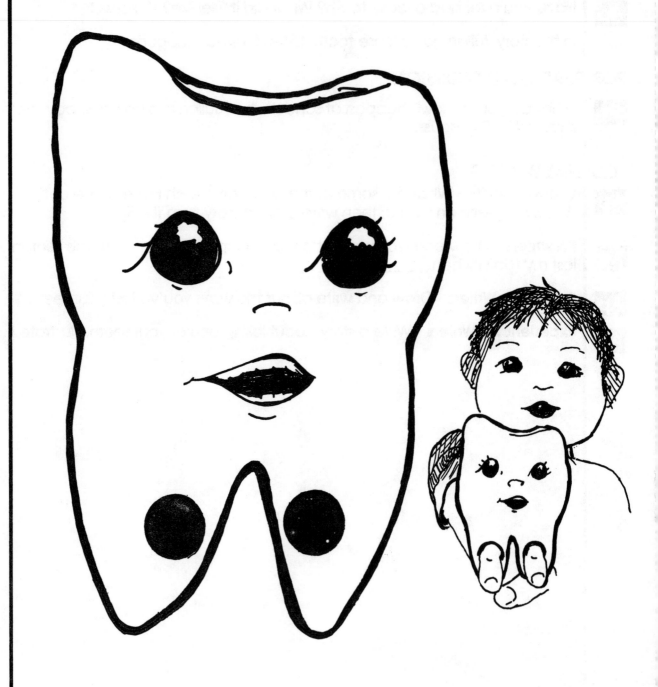

Name _____

THE STORIES JULIAN TELLS

Ap
Beginning Writers

Make a sign advertising your own cave tooth.

Name _____

THE STORIES JULIAN TELLS

How would you help Julian lose a tooth?

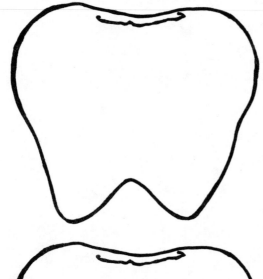

I would _____

_____

_____ .

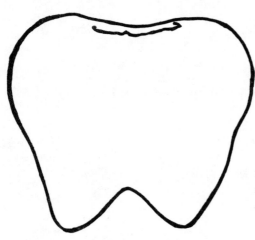

I would _____

_____

_____ .

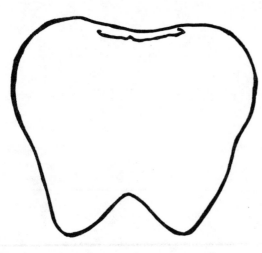

I would _____

_____

_____ .

Name _____

THE STORIES JULIAN TELLS

GLORIA WHO MIGHT BE MY BEST FRIEND

PREREADING DISCUSSION:

 How do you go about making a good friend? (Discuss.)

Julian makes a new friend in this story. See how he does it.

POSTREADING DISCUSSION:

 What do you think would have happened if Gloria had laughed at Julian when he fell doing a cartwheel? Why?

JOURNAL WRITING:

 Group Activity - What are some other wishes Julian and Gloria might wish? (Draw/write on board. Model writing sentences they would have put on their kite tail.)

 Prewriters - Draw your wishes. Copy and complete this sentence, "I would wish for _____ ."

 Beginning Writers - Draw and write what your wishes would be.

 Experienced Writers - Write everything you would wish for. Illustrate your writing.

THE STORIES JULIAN TELLS

Draw what is in this moving van.

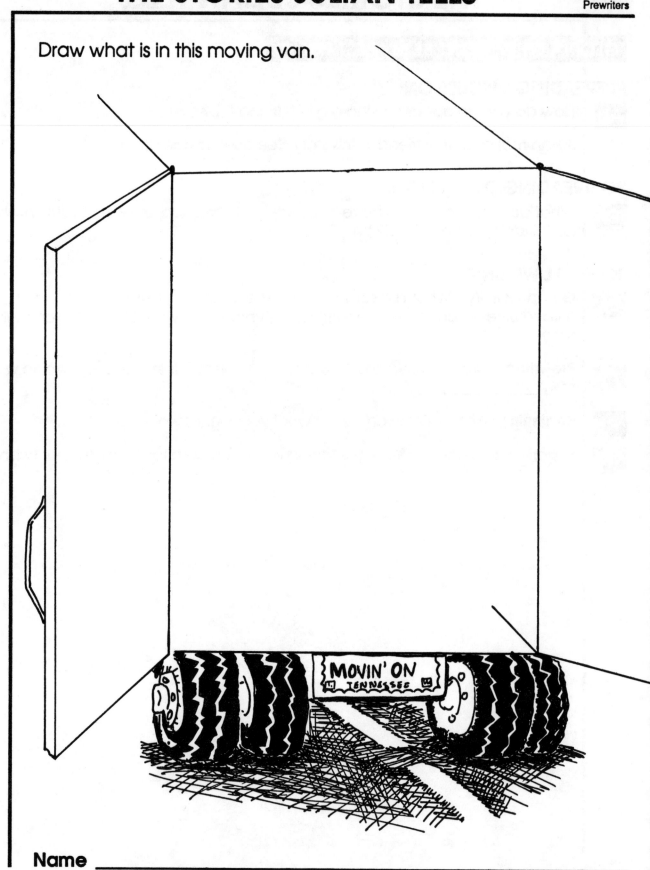

Name _____

THE STORIES JULIAN TELLS

Beginning Writers

What things of yours would you show a new friend?

I would show my _____

_____ .

I would show my _____

_____ .

I would show my _____

_____ .

Name _____

THE STORIES JULIAN TELLS

Decorate your kite. Don't forget to put your wishes on it.

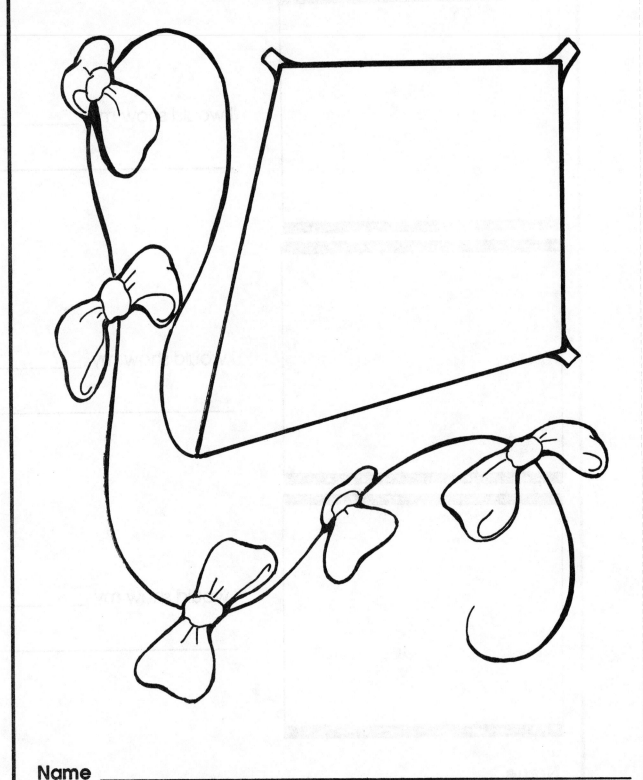

THE STORIES JULIAN TELLS

MATH

MEASURING/COOKING:
Make lemon pudding.

GRAPH HEIGHT:
Measure and graph growth of plants in the class garden.

SCIENCE

GARDEN:
Plant a small class garden in milk cartons and other containers. Learn about plants.

TASTING PARTY:
Taste things mentioned in the book — lemon pudding, figs, beans, corn. Then describe them.

SOCIAL STUDIES

PUNISHMENT:
Was the father's punishment in "The Pudding Like A Night on the Sea" fair? Why or why not? What kind of punishment(s) do you get? Are they fair? Why or why not?

FAMILIES:
Discuss how Julian's family works together and solves problems.
Compare/contrast to your family.

FINE ARTS

STRAW BLOW TREES:
Put a glob of brown paint on paper and blow it around with a straw to make a tree trunk with branches. Decorate it with tissue blossoms, leaves, or fruit.

DIORAMA:
Construct dioramas of favorite Julian stories.

KITE:
Make colorful kites.

LANGUAGE ARTS

CATALOG CATS:
Put together a class catalog of cats or pets, with pictures and descriptions of each.

PUPPET SHOW:
In small groups, do a puppet show about losing teeth.

THE LITTLES

CHAPTERS 1, 2, 3, and 4

PREREADING DISCUSSION:

 What do you think it would be like to be little? What things could you do? Where could you live?

This is a book about the Littles, a family of very small people. Listen to what they do and where they live.

POSTREADING DISCUSSION:

 How do the Littles help the Biggs? (Discuss.)

JOURNAL WRITING:

 Group Activity - If you were little, how would you help your family? (Draw/write student responses. Model writing sentences from the information. Encourage them to be creative in their own writing.)

 Prewriters - Draw how you would help your family. Copy and complete this sentence, "I would help my family by _____ ."

 Beginning Writers - Draw and write the ways you would help your family.

 Experienced Writers - Write about the ways you would help your family. Illustrate your writing.

THE LITTLES

Draw your favorite meal. What would the Littles' meal look like?

My Meal

The Littles' Meal

THE LITTLES

Draw the Littles to size.

6 —
½ —
5 —
½ —
4 —
½ —
3 —
½ —
2 —
½ —
1 —
½ —

6 —
½ —
5 —
I'm
sooooo
taɪɪɪ!
4 —
½ —
3 —
½ —
YELLOW
2 —
½ —
1 —
½ —

We know how tall
these Littles are.

Mr. Little - 6 in.
Lucy - 3 3/4 in.
Tom - 4 1/2 in.

How tall do you think
these Littles are?

Mrs. Little _____
Uncle Pete _____
Granny _____

Name _____

THE LITTLES

If you were a Little, what would you do with the red socks?

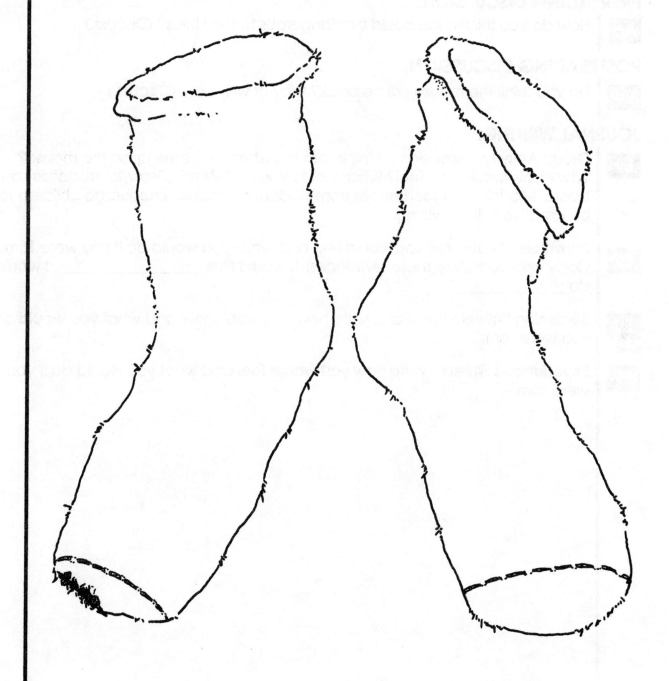

I would _____.

Name _____

THE LITTLES

CHAPTERS 5 and 6

PREREADING DISCUSSION:

Ap How do you think mice could be dangerous to the Littles? (Discuss.)

POSTREADING DISCUSSION:

Ev Do you think the mouse will be back? Why or why not? (Discuss.)

JOURNAL WRITING:

Ev **Group Activity -** How do you think Tom felt when he came upon the mouse? Why? How would you feel? What would you do? Why? (Draw/list responses on board. Model writing sentences from student responses. Encourage children to be creative in their writing.)

Ev **Prewriters -** Draw how you would feel and what you would do if you were Tom. Copy and complete these sentences: "I would feel _____ . I would do _____ .

Ev **Beginning Writers -** Draw and write how you would feel and what you would do if you were Tom.

Ev **Experienced Writers -** Write how you would feel and what you would do if you were Tom.

THE LITTLES

What do you think Mrs. Newcombe's story is about? Draw the beginning, middle, and end.

Name _____

THE LITTLES

If you were one of the Littles, what would you use for furniture?

I would use _____ for _____ .

I would use _____ for _____ .

I would use _____ for _____ .

Name _____

THE LITTLES

How are the Newcombes different from the Biggs?

Name _____

THE LITTLES

CHAPTERS 7 and 8

PREREADING DISCUSSION:

 How do you think the Little family feels about the mice? Why? What do you think they will do? Why? (Discuss.)

Listen to the way each person in the Little family acts in these chapters.

POSTREADING DISCUSSION:

 How did each person in the Little family act? (Draw/list on board.)

Tom   Lucy   Mr. Little   Mrs. Little   Uncle Pete   Granny

JOURNAL WRITING:

 Group Activity - Think of words to describe each Little character. (Write on board.) Which character is most like you? (Discuss. Then model writing sentences using what was written on the board and what was discussed.)

 Prewriters - Draw how one of the Little characters is most like you. Copy and complete this sentence, "_____ is most like me because _____."

 Beginning Writers - Draw and write which character is most like you and why.

 Experienced Writers - Write which Little character is most like you and why.

THE LITTLES

Ap/Ev
Prewriters

What Halloween costume would you wear if you were a Little?

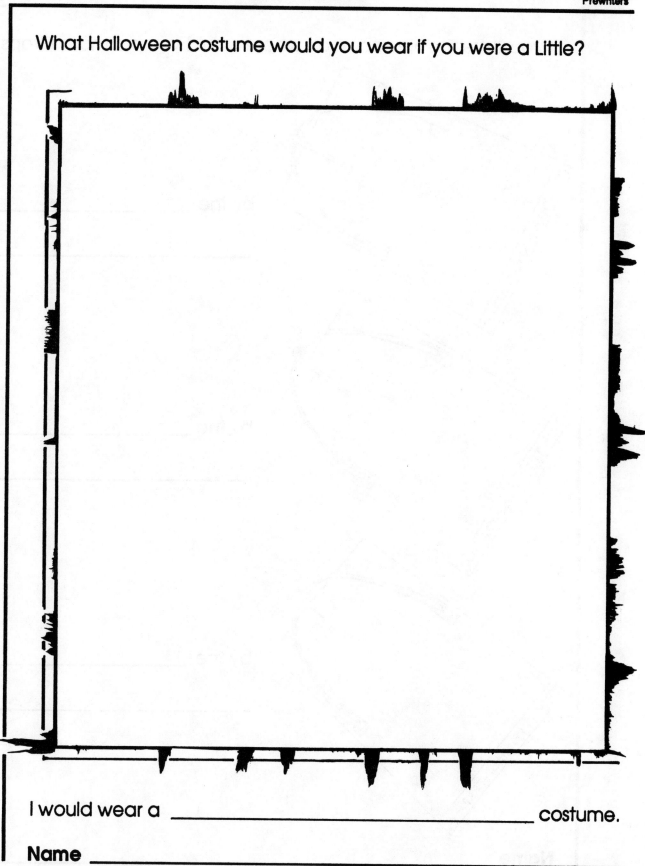

I would wear a _____ costume.

Name _____

THE LITTLES

If you were the Newcombes, where would you put mouse traps?

TRIP-TRAP-MOUSE-TRAP

by the _____

_____

TRIP-TRAP-MOUSE-TRAP

by the _____

_____

TRIP-TRAP-MOUSE-TRAP

by the _____

_____

Name _____

THE LITTLES

What do you think would happen if a real mouse saw Tom in his mouse costume?

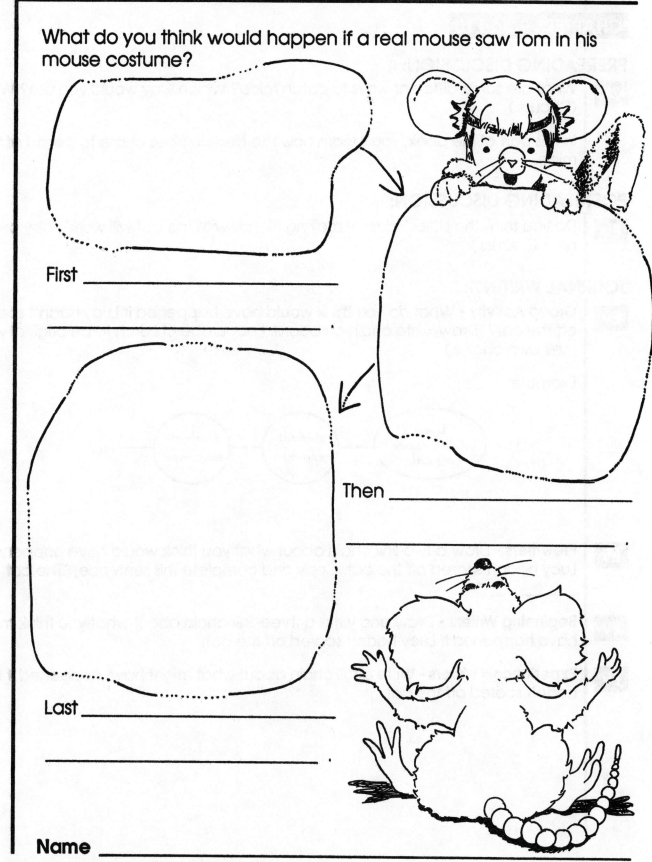

First _____

Then _____

_____

Last _____

_____

Name _____

THE LITTLES

CHAPTERS 9 and 10

PREREADING DISCUSSION:

K/Ap What are some different ways to catch mice? Which way would you use? Why? (Discuss.)

In this part of the book, you'll learn how the Newcombes chose to get rid of the mice.

POSTREADING DISCUSSION:

Ev Do you think the Littles' idea of making friends with the cat will work? Why or why not? (Discuss.)

JOURNAL WRITING:

Ev **Group Activity** - What do you think would have happened if Lucy hadn't scared off the cat? (Draw/write chain on board. Encourage children to be original with their own chains.)

Example:

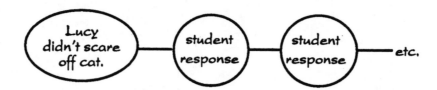

Ev **Prewriters** - Draw a two-link chain about what you think would have happened if Lucy hadn't scared off the cat. Copy and complete this sentence, "The cat _____."

Ev **Beginning Writers** - Draw and write a three-link chain about what you think might have happened if Lucy hadn't scared off the cat.

Ev **Experienced Writers** - Write a full chain about what might have happened if Lucy hadn't scared off the cat.

THE LITTLES

How would you make friends with the cat?

I would _____

Name _____

THE LITTLES

What would you do in your house that you would blame on the cat?

I would _____

_____

Name _____

THE LITTLES

If you were little, where would your hiding place be in your house?

THE LITTLES

CHAPTER 11

PREREADING DISCUSSION:

 How would you feel if you were little and about to make friends with a big cat? (Discuss.)

Listen to how the characters feel in the last part of the book.

POSTREADING DISCUSSION:

 What things do cats like people to do? What kinds of things do you think the Littles can do for the cat? (Discuss.)

JOURNAL WRITING:

 Group Activity - What do you think Tom might do to get the Biggs to keep the cat? What would you do? (Draw/write list on board. Then model writing sentences from it. Encourage children to be original with their own writing.)

 Prewriters - Draw what you would do to get the Biggs to keep the cat. Copy and complete this sentence, "I would _____ ."

 Beginning Writers - Draw and write what you would do to get the Biggs to keep the cat.

 Experienced Writers - Write a story about what you would do to get the Biggs to keep the cat.

THE LITTLES

Draw yourself riding the cat. Draw where you are going.

I am going _____.

Name _____

THE LITTLES

What would you say to the cat?

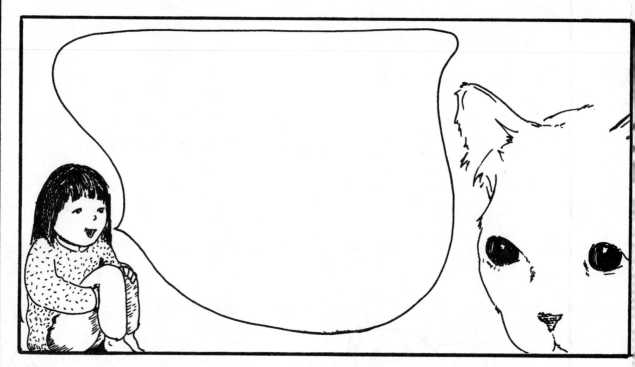

What would the cat do?

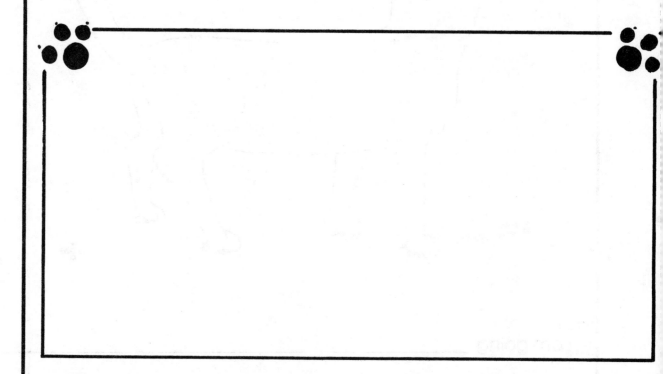

Name _____

THE LITTLES

Cut out and fold the booklet. Write and draw how you would tame a cat.

← fold

How to Tame a CAT

by: _____

THE LITTLES

MATH

MEASURING:
Measure the height of the Littles (no more than 6 inches tall). Then find or bring in things they could use, e.g., spool for a table, and measure them.

GRAPH:
Graph heights of the children in class.

SCIENCE

CATS AND MICE:
Learn about cats and mice.

SOUP CAN ELEVATOR:
Construct a soup can elevator using spool pulleys as pictured in chapter 7.

SOCIAL STUDIES

FAMILIES:
Compare and contrast the Little family with your family.

CATS IN HISTORY:
Learn about cats in ancient Egypt and throughout history.

FINE ARTS

DIORAMA:
Construct dioramas of the Littles' house and other things mentioned in the story.

SEWING PUPPETS:
Sew sock puppets of favorite characters in the book.

LANGUAGE ARTS

PUPPET SHOW:
In small groups, act out events in the story with puppets or make up your own stories.

STORY:
Make up a story Mrs. Newcombe might have written.

ANOTHER STORY:
In small groups, make up stories about how the Littles will get the Biggs to keep the cat.

LAFCADIO, THE LION WHO SHOT BACK

CHAPTERS 1 and 2

PREREADING DISCUSSION:

 Do you like the sound of the word "marshmallow"? Do you like the sounds of the words "tapioca" and "gumbo"? What other words do you like the sounds of? (Discuss.)

In this part of the book, Lafcadio likes the sound of a word and has a new experience. Listen to what happens.

POSTREADING DISCUSSION:

 Why do you think Lafcadio wants to be such a good shot?

JOURNAL WRITING:

 Group Activity - What do you think would have happened if the hunter had shot Lafcadio? ("Chain" responses. Encourage children to be creative when doing their own chains.)

Example:

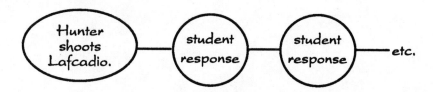

 Prewriters - Draw one or two links of your own chain. Copy and complete these sentences: "Lafcadio _____ . The hunter _____ ."

 Beginning Writers - Draw and write a three-link chain about what would happen if the hunter shot Lafcadio.

 Experienced Writers - Write a complete original chain of events.

LAFCADIO, THE LION WHO SHOT BACK

Draw some things Lafcadio could shoot for practice.

Name _____

LAFCADIO, THE LION WHO SHOT BACK

What would Lafcadio think about if he were a rug in front of the fireplace?

Name _____

LAFCADIO, THE LION WHO SHOT BACK

An Experienced Writers

How is Lafcadio the same as and different from other lions?

Same   Different

LAFCADIO, THE LION WHO SHOT BACK

CHAPTERS 3 and 4

PREREADING DISCUSSION:

An How many different ways do you think Lafcadio might learn to shoot his gun? (Discuss.)

Listen for all the different ways he learns how to shoot. See if he uses any of your ideas.

POSTREADING DISCUSSION:

Ev Do you think the circus man will really give Lafcadio marshmallows and keep his promise? Why or why not? (Discuss.)

(Mind Teaser: How do you think the circus man learned about Lafcadio if all the hunters and finder-outers were shot?)

JOURNAL WRITING:

Sy **Group Activity** - Read and chant the "Marshmallow Song" in chapter 4 beginning with "Marshmallows, Marshmallows..." and ending "Marshy-Mushy--." Make up your own marshmallow song. (Write on board.)

C **Prewriters** - Draw a picture of a portion of the marshmallow song, and copy an appropriate sentence from it off the board.

Sy **Beginning Writers** - Draw and write your own marshmallow song.

Sy **Experienced Writers** - Write your own marshmallow song. Illustrate it.

LAFCADIO, THE LION WHO SHOT BACK

Sy
Prewriters

What do you think a marshmallow house would look like?

LAFCADIO, THE LION WHO SHOT BACK

Beginning Writers

If Lafcadio had a suitcase, what do you think he would pack?

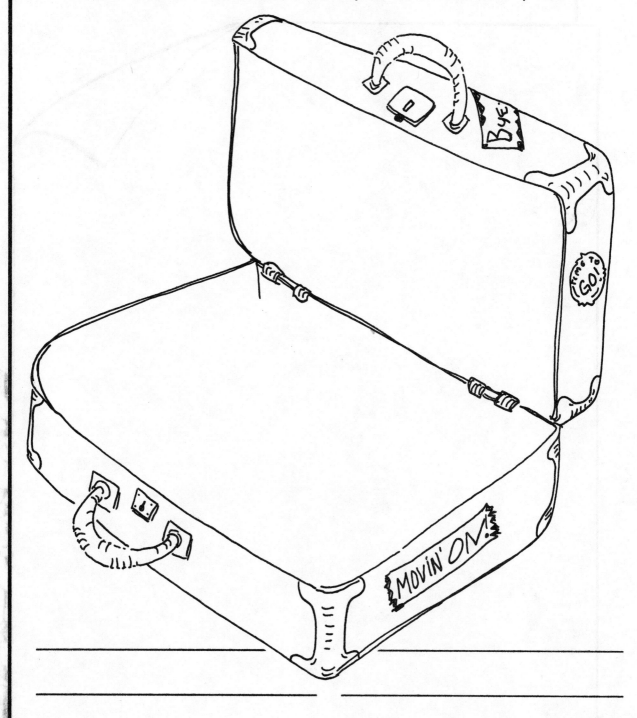

Name _____

LAFCADIO, THE LION WHO SHOT BACK

Sy
Experienced Writers

Make a poster the circus man might use to tell about Lafcadio.

Name _____

LAFCADIO, THE LION WHO SHOT BACK

CHAPTERS 5 and 6

PREREADING DISCUSSION:

An What new things do you think Lafcadio will see in the city that he'd never seen before? What new experiences might he have? (Draw/list on board.)

Example: Sees   Experiences

_____   _____

_____   _____

Listen to what he sees and the experiences he has.

POSTREADING DISCUSSION:

An What new things did Lafcadio see? What new things did he experience? (Circle correct responses and list new ones.)

Example: Sees   Experiences

_____   _____

_____   _____

JOURNAL WRITING:

An **Group Activity** - How is a city different from a jungle? (Draw/write contrasts. Encourage children to be original with their responses.)

Example: City   Jungle

_____   _____

_____   _____

(Model using this information in sentence form.)

An **Prewriters** - Draw how a city is different from the jungle. Copy and complete these sentences: "A city is _____ . The jungle is _____ ."

An **Beginning Writers** - Draw and write at least two ways a city is different from the jungle.

An **Experienced Writers** - Write as many ways as you can think of that a city is different from a jungle. Illustrate your ideas.

LAFCADIO, THE LION WHO SHOT BACK

What toys do you think Lafcadio would like in the bathtub?

He would like _____ .

Name _____

LAFCADIO, THE LION WHO SHOT BACK

Fill in the comic strip.

Name _____

LAFCADIO, THE LION WHO SHOT BACK

If you were Lafcadio, what else (besides elevators) would you like about the city?

I would _____

_____

_____ .

I would _____

_____

_____ .

I would _____

_____

_____ .

Name _____

LAFCADIO, THE LION WHO SHOT BACK

CHAPTERS 7 and 8

PREREADING DISCUSSION:

Ap When you are getting ready to go somewhere special, what do you do? (Encourage responses about personal grooming, e.g., comb hair, dress up.) What do you order when you go out to a nice dinner?

In this part of the story, Lafcadio gets ready for the circus and goes out to dinner. Listen to what happens.

POSTREADING DISCUSSION:

Ev How do you think Lafcadio felt about the melted marshmallow suit? Do you think he ever thought about eating anybody? Why?

JOURNAL WRITING:

Ap **Group Activity -** If you went to the restaurant with Lafcadio, what would you order to eat? (Draw/list on board. Model writing sentences using information from the list.)

Ap **Prewriters -** Draw what you would have ordered for dinner and dessert. Copy and complete this sentence, "I would want to eat _____ ."

Ap **Beginning Writers -** Draw and write what you would want to eat.

Ap **Experienced Writers -** Write about the dinner and dessert you would have ordered. Illustrate your writing.

LAFCADIO, THE LION WHO SHOT BACK

Cut out Lafcadio and give him a good haircut. Then paste him on a paper bag and make him a puppet.

Name _____

LAFCADIO, THE LION WHO SHOT BACK

An
Beginning Writers

What are some other silly ways to cook marshmallows?

Marshmallow _____

_____

_____ .

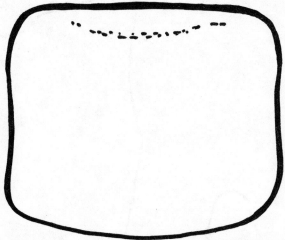

Marshmallow _____

_____

_____ .

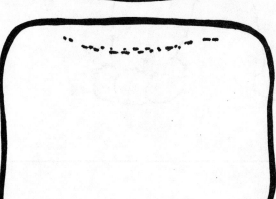

Marshmallow _____

_____

_____ .

Name _____

LAFCADIO, THE LION WHO SHOT BACK

Design a suit for Lafcadio. Describe it.

_____

_____.

Name _____

LAFCADIO, THE LION WHO SHOT BACK

CHAPTERS 9, 10, and 11

PREREADING DISCUSSION:

An What would you do and where would you go if you were rich and famous? What would it feel like? (Discuss.)

Lafcadio becomes rich and famous in the last part of the book. See what he does, where he goes, and how he feels.

POSTREADING DISCUSSION:

Ev Where do you think Lafcadio went? What is he doing? Is he happy? (Discuss.)

JOURNAL WRITING:

Sy **Group Activity** - If you knew where Lafcadio was, what would you want to ask him? (Draw/write children's phrases. Model writing sentences from them. Encourage children to be original with their own writing.)

C/Ap **Prewriters** - Draw a picture and copy a short letter from the board.

Sy **Beginning Writers** - Draw a picture and write a letter to Lafcadio.

Sy **Experienced Writers** - Write a letter to Lafcadio. Draw a picture to go with it.

LAFCADIO, THE LION WHO SHOT BACK

What would you pack to go to Africa?

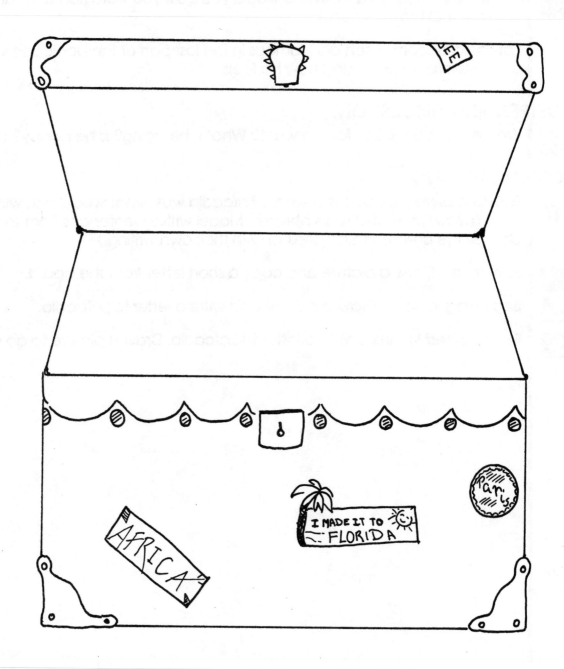

Name _____

LAFCADIO, THE LION WHO SHOT BACK

Follow the directions and map Lafcadio's journeys.

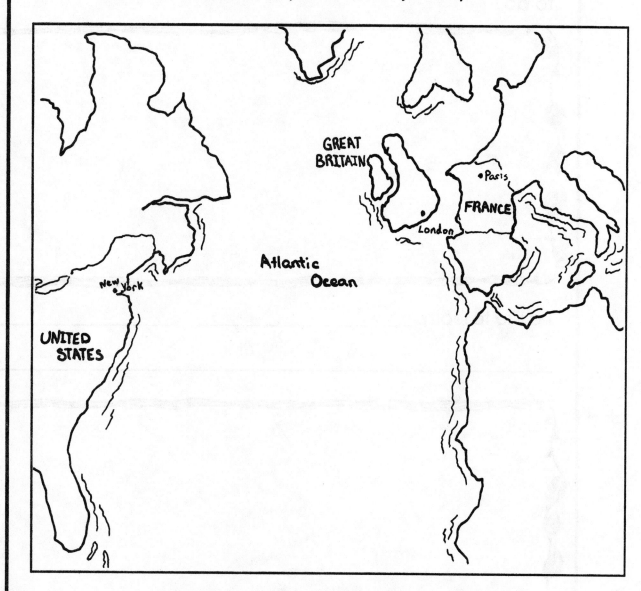

1. Draw a line from <u>New York</u> to <u>London</u>.
2. Color Great Britain yellow.
3. Draw a line from <u>London</u> to <u>Paris</u>.
4. Color France red.
5. Draw a line from <u>Paris</u> to <u>New York</u>.
6. Color the United States green.
7. Color the Atlantic Ocean blue.

Name _____

LAFCADIO, THE LION WHO SHOT BACK

Ev
Experienced Writers

If you were Lafcadio, what are some things you'd want to learn to do?

I'd like to learn _____

_____.

I'd like to learn _____

_____.

Name _____

LAFCADIO, THE LION WHO SHOT BACK

MATH

100 BANGS:
Chant and count the 100 bangs Lafcadio did in chapter 9.

SCIENCE

TASTING PARTY:
Taste Lafcadio's favorite foods: marshmallows, jam, and buttermilk. Describe them. Compare and contrast the flavors.

SOCIAL STUDIES

COMPARE/CONTRAST:
Compare and contrast Lafcadio's life-style between the jungle and the city.

MAPPING:
Construct a class map of Lafcadio's travels. Learn about those places.

FINE ARTS

MARSHMALLOW ART:
See what creations you can come up with when given marshmallows and toothpicks. Work either in groups or individually.

DIORAMA:
Make dioramas of favorite parts of the stories.

LANGUAGE ARTS

WHERE IS LAFCADIO?
Write newspaper stories and TV and radio ads asking the whereabouts of Lafcadio and reporting on supposed sightings of him.

CHANT:
Sing/chant the "Marshmallow Song" in chapter 4 and/or "Two, Four, Six, Eight" in chapter 9.

AUTOGRAPH SIGNING:
Practice signing your own autograph with your right hand, then left hand, then both hands at once like Lafcadio did.

RAMONA AND HER FATHER

CHAPTER 1

PREREADING DISCUSSION:

Ev How can you tell if someone in your family is unhappy?

In this chapter, someone in Ramona's family is unhappy. See how she finds out.

POSTREADING DISCUSSION:

Ev What do you think Ramona can do to help her family? (List on board.)

Example: no allowance

help cook

don't ask for toys

take lunch to school, etc.

JOURNAL WRITING:

Ap **Group Activity** - Using the postreading list generated on the board, write a chart story about what Ramona could do to help her family now that her father is out of work.

Ev **Prewriters** - Draw what you would do to help your family if you were Ramona. Copy and complete this sentence, "I would help my family by _____ ."

Ev **Beginning Writers** - Draw and write what you would do to help your family if you were Ramona.

Ev **Experienced Writers** - Write a story about what you would do to help your family if you were Ramona. Illustrate your story.

RAMONA AND HER FATHER

Ap
Prewriters

Draw the things you want for Christmas.

Name _____

RAMONA AND HER FATHER

Where is your favorite place to eat?
What do you order when you eat there?

strawberry ice cream + jelly beans + potato chips + milk + liver and onions + potatoes + pop +

raisins + pretzels + crawfish + oatmeal + tofu + rice + roasted pumpkin seeds + boiled peanuts + soup +

+ food + chocolate candy + french fries + apple pie + cookies + brocoli + snack cakes + chicken + jello

+ Chili + barbeque + coolwhip + lemon pie + grapes + quiche + pancakes + squash + fish sticks + carrots +

My favorite place to eat is _____.

I order _____.

Name _____

RAMONA AND HER FATHER

Ev
Experienced Writers

Make a list of what you want for Christmas.

Name _____

RAMONA AND HER FATHER

CHAPTER 2

PREREADING DISCUSSION:

An | What could you do to make one million dollars?

Ramona thinks she's found a way in this chapter.

POSTREADING DISCUSSION:

Ev | If you were Mr. Quimby, how would you feel about having a daughter like Ramona? Why? (Discuss.)

JOURNAL WRITING:

Ap | **Group Activity -** How would you make one million dollars? What would you buy for your family? (Draw/list on board. Model writing sentences using listed phrases on board.)

Ap | **Prewriters -** Draw how you would make one million dollars for your family and what you would buy with it. Copy and complete these sentences: "I would make one million dollars by _____ . I would spend it on _____ ."

Ap | **Beginning Writers -** Draw and write how you would make one million dollars for your family.

Ap | **Experienced Writers -** Write what would you do to make one million dollars and what you would buy for your family. Illustrate your writing.

RAMONA AND HER FATHER

What would you buy for your family if you had one million dollars?

Name _____

RAMONA AND HER FATHER

Draw your favorite TV commercials. Write what they are.

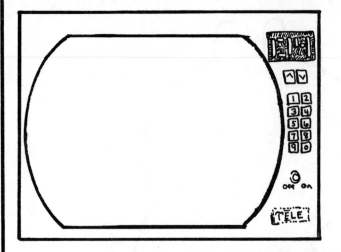

I like the _____

commercial because _____

_____ .

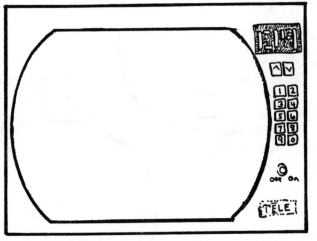

I like the _____

commercial because _____

_____ .

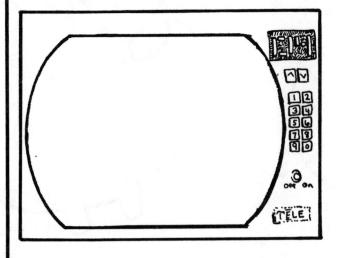

I like the _____

commercial because _____

_____ .

Name _____

RAMONA AND HER FATHER

Draw and write a commercial you'd like to do on TV.

_____

_____

_____

_____

_____

_____

_____

Name _____

RAMONA AND HER FATHER

CHAPTER 3

PREREADING DISCUSSION:

 What kinds of things do you do to cheer people up when they're unhappy? Do they always work? Why or why not?

In this chapter, Ramona tries to cheer everybody up. See if it works.

POSTREADING DISCUSSION:

 What other kinds of things do you think Ramona worries about? (List on board.)

Example: Ramona
             Will Dad's lungs turn black?
             Will the cat starve?
             Will they really get another pumpkin for Halloween?
             Will Dad ever get a job?
             Will Mom and Dad ever be happy again?

JOURNAL WRITING:

 Group Activity - What do you worry about? Circle things from the postreading activity that children in class say they worry about. List other things. Model writing sentences from class-generated ideas.)

Ramona	Our Class
Will Dad's lungs turn black?	
Will the cat starve?	
Will they really get another pumpkin for Halloween?	
Will Dad ever get a job?	
Will Mom and Dad ever be happy again?	

Sy **Prewriters** - Draw some things you worry about. Copy and complete this sentence, "I worry about _____ ."

Sy **Beginning Writers** - Draw and write about the kinds of things you worry about.

Sy **Experienced Writers** - Write about the kinds of things you worry about. Illustrate your writing.

RAMONA AND HER FATHER

Draw your own jack-o-lantern.

Draw what it would look like if the cat ate part of it.

Name _____

RAMONA AND HER FATHER

What special toy do you sleep with or would sleep with if you wanted to?

My special toy is a _____ .

I feel better when I sleep with it because _____

_____ .

Name _____

RAMONA AND HER FATHER

What do you think everyone wanted to say at breakfast but didn't?

Name _____

RAMONA AND HER FATHER

CHAPTER 4

PREREADING DISCUSSION:

Ap Have you ever tried to get someone to break a bad habit? What did you do?

In this chapter, Ramona tries to get her father to break a bad habit.

POSTREADING DISCUSSION:

Ev Do you think Mr. Quimby will really stop smoking? Why or why not? (Discuss.)

JOURNAL WRITING:

Ap **Group Activity -** Why should Mr. Quimby stop smoking? (Write on the board the reasons children give for Mr. Quimby to quit smoking. Then model writing sentences using their ideas.)

Ap **Prewriters -** Draw a poster for Mr. Quimby to help him stop smoking. Copy and complete this sentence, "Stop smoking because _____."

Ap **Beginning Writers -** Draw and write some more no smoking signs Ramona might make.

Ap **Experienced Writers -** Write a letter urging Mr. Quimby to quit smoking. Illustrate your letter.

RAMONA AND HER FATHER

Draw a "big and important" thing you would want to do if you were Ramona.

Name _____

RAMONA AND HER FATHER

Where would you put these no smoking signs?

I would put it on _____

_____ .

It will go on the _____

_____ .

This sign will be on _____

_____ .

I will put this on _____

_____ .

Name _____

RAMONA AND HER FATHER

Make a colorful no smoking sign for Mr. Quimby.

Name _____

RAMONA AND HER FATHER

CHAPTER 5

PREREADING DISCUSSION:

Ev | What are some things you do that make you feel good? (Discuss.)

Ramona does some things in this chapter that make her feel good. See if some of them are similar to what you do to feel good.

POSTREADING DISCUSSION:

C | What did Ramona do that made her feel better? How are her ways the same as and different from yours? (Discuss.)

JOURNAL WRITING:

An | **Group Activity** - How are you the same as and different from Ramona? (List on board.)

Same	Different
_____	_____
_____	_____
_____	_____

An | **Prewriters** - Draw how you and Ramona are the same and how you are different. Copy and complete these sentences. "Ramona and I are the same because _____ . We are different because _____ ."

An | **Beginning Writers** - Draw and write how you and Ramona are the same and how you are different.

An | **Experienced Writers** - Write about the ways you and Ramona are the same and how you are different. Illustrate your writing.

RAMONA AND HER FATHER

Make your own tin can stilts.

1.

Punch two holes near the bottom of 2 two-pound coffee cans.

2.

Cut two pieces of heavy string 4 feet long.

3.

Put the string through the holes. Tie them to make a loop.

4.

Hold the string tight. Walk on your stilts.

Name _____

RAMONA AND HER FATHER

Ev
Beginning Writers

What are some ways you like to make noise?

I like to _____

_____ .

I like to _____

_____ .

I like to _____

_____ .

I like to _____

_____ .

Name _____

RAMONA AND HER FATHER

Write the song you would sing on your stilts if you were Ramona.

_____

_____

_____

_____

_____

_____

_____

_____

Name _____

RAMONA AND HER FATHER

CHAPTER 6

PREREADING DISCUSSION:

Ap Have you ever volunteered your mother or someone else in your family to do something before you asked him/her? What happened?

Ramona does that in this chapter. See what happens to her.

POSTREADING DISCUSSION:

Ev How would this chapter have been different if Ramona hadn't volunteered to be a sheep? ("Chain" on board.)

Example:

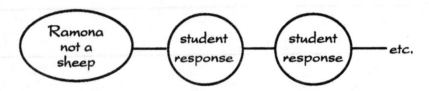

JOURNAL WRITING:

Ap **Group Activity** - Create a chart story from the chain you just put together. (Write chart story on board.)

Sy **Prewriters** - Draw two links of your own chain about what would happen if Ramona hadn't volunteered to be a sheep.

Sy **Beginning Writers** - Draw and write three links of your own chain about how this chapter would have been different if Ramona hadn't volunteered to be a sheep.

Sy **Experienced Writers** - Write your own chain about how this chapter would have been different if Ramona hadn't volunteered to be a sheep. Illustrate your writing.

RAMONA AND HER FATHER

Draw what each person in your family does to make a happy family.

Name _____

RAMONA AND HER FATHER

Why do you think Ramona is a spoiled brat?
Is she well-behaved? Draw and write your answers.

Spoiled Brat

Well-Behaved

Name _____

RAMONA AND HER FATHER

An
Experienced Writers

How would you make a sheep suit?

First I'd _____

_____.

Then I'd _____

_____.

Next I'd _____

_____.

Last I'd _____

_____.

Name _____

RAMONA AND HER FATHER

CHAPTER 7

PREREADING DISCUSSION:

Ev Do you think Mr. Quimby got Ramona's sheep suit done in time? Why or why not?

Let's see what happens.

POSTREADING DISCUSSION:

Ev What do you think made the "magic" Ramona felt?

JOURNAL WRITING:

Ap **Group Activity** - What are some "magic" times you've had with your family? (List responses on board. Model writing sentences from student ideas. Encourage children to be original with their own writing.)

Ap **Prewriters** - Draw a special, magical time you had with your family. Copy and complete this sentence, "I had a special, magical time with my family when _____."

Ap **Beginning Writers -** Draw and write about a special time you had with your family.

Ap **Experienced Writers -** Write a story about a magical time you had with your family. Illustrate your writing.

RAMONA AND HER FATHER

Draw how you would look in a sheep suit.

I would look like a _____.

Name _____

RAMONA AND HER FATHER

What presents do you think Ramona will get? Why?

She got a _____   She got a _____

because _____   because _____

_____ .   _____ .

Name _____

RAMONA AND HER FATHER

Decorate, cut out, and write a card to send to Ramona. Make the other one for someone special.

fold

Name _____

RAMONA AND HER FATHER

MATH

MEASURING/COOKING:
Make pumpkin pie and other recipes out of pumpkin.

SCIENCE

SIMILARITIES/DIFFERENCES:
Discuss families and how every family is different.

SOCIAL STUDIES

HEALTH:
Learn about the hazards of smoking.

FINE ARTS

MURAL:
Draw a long picture of some aspect of the story, like Ramona and her father did.

LANGUAGE ARTS

LETTER:
Write a letter from Ramona to her father explaining her feelings.

INTERVIEW:
Interview an older person like Beezus, as Ramona did with Mrs. Swink. Find out what this person did when he/she was a young child.

Annotated Bibliography

WORDLESS BOOKS

Anno's Alphabet - Mitsumasa Anno, Harper & Row, 1974.
Each wooden letter presents a slight optical illusion. Brilliantly executed, this book is a joy to look at over and over again.

Bobo's Dream - Martha Alexander, Dial, 1970.
Bobo's young master retrieves his bone from a larger dog who had stolen it. Grateful, Bobo dreams of helping the boy.

Deep In The Forest - Brinton Turkle, Dutton, 1976.
This story is a delightful twist on "The Three Bears." A bear cub invades a family's cabin, eats the food, breaks the furniture, and ruffles the beds.

PICTURE BOOKS

Alexander, Who Used To Be Rich Last Sunday - Judith Viorst, Atheneum, 1978.
Alexander's grandparents gave him a dollar last Sunday. There is so much to spend it on, it gradually finds its way out of his pockets.

East O' The Sun And West O' The Moon - Mercer Mayer, Viking Press, 1966.
A maiden enlists the help of the Moon, Father Forest, Great Fish, and North Wind to rescue a youth taken to a distant troll kingdom.

The Elephant's Child - Rudyard Kipling, HBJ Press, 1983.
Because the elephant's child is curious about what the crocodile has for dinner, his nose gets pulled into the long trunk all elephants have today.

Fish Is Fish - Leo Lionni, Alfred A. Knopf, 1970.
When a fish jumps out of his pond to see the world his frog friend has described, he learns the true beauty of his own world.

The Girl Who Loved Wild Horses - Paul Goble, Bradbury, 1979.
Carried away in a stampede, a Plains Indian girl loves the freedom of the wild horses and chooses to stay with them.

Green Eggs And Ham - Dr. Seuss, Random House, 1960.
In this Seuss classic, Sam-I-Am tries everything in his power to get a friend to taste green eggs and ham.

A House Is A House For Me - Mary Ann Hoberman, Viking, 1978.
Houses for animals, houses for things — houses are the subject of this delightful rhyme, which is brimming with images and energy.

The Island Of The Skog - Steven Kellogg, Dial, 1973.
A group of mice try to scare the only Skog off its island and learn that kindness is the best way to approach someone new.

Milton The Early Riser - Robert Kraus, Simon & Schuster, 1972.
Milton wakes up early, but everyone is still asleep. He amuses himself and works so hard that when everyone wakes up, he is fast asleep.

Molly's Pilgrim - Barbara Cohen; Lothrop, Lee, and Shepard; 1983.
Asked to make a pilgrim doll for Thanksgiving, Molly's mother makes a doll that looks like herself when she left Russia in search of religious freedom.

Nana Upstairs And Nana Downstairs - Tomie de Paola, Putnam, 1973.
Tommy has a special relationship with his Nanas, a grandmother and a great-grandmother. When they die, he learns to accept their deaths.

A New Coat For Anna - Harriet Ziefert, Alfred A. Knopf, 1986.
Times are hard after the war, so Anna's mother trades precious items for the wool, spinning, weaving, and tailoring of her daughter's new coat.

Once A Mouse - Marcia Brown, Scribner's, 1962.
When a hermit saves the life of a mouse by turning it into a cat, a dog, and a tiger, it gets increasingly vain.

One Fine Day - Nonny Hogrogian, Macmillan, 1972.
A classic story about the chain of events a fox goes through to get his tail back after losing it while stealing some milk.

The Paper Bag Princess - Robert N. Munsch; Annick Press, Ltd.; 1980.
After a dragon burns Princess Elizabeth's clothes and carries off Prince Ronald, Princess Elizabeth wears only a paper bag as she sets off to rescue Prince Ronald.

The Paper Crane - Molly Bang, Greenwillow Books, 1985.
A restaurant owner's generosity to a stranger is repaid with a magical paper crane.

Stevie - John Steptoe, Harper & Row, 1969.
When young Stevie comes to stay with Robert, he always seems to get in the way. Even so, when Stevie leaves, Robert misses him.

There's A Nightmare In My Closet - Mercer Mayer, Dial, 1968.
A boy finally confronts the nightmare in his closet and learns it isn't as terrifying as he thought.

The Third Story Cat - Leslie Baker; Little, Brown & Company; 1987.
Alice is an apartment cat who escapes for a day of fun and intrigue in the park across the street.

Too Many Books! - Caroline Feller Bauer; Frederick Warne & Company, Inc.; 1984.
When Maralou ends up with too many books, she starts giving them away. This action sparks the town's interest in reading, and the enthusiasm spreads.

Whistle For Willie - Ezra Jack Keats, Viking Press, 1964.
Peter wants to learn how to whistle to call his dog Willie. He tries and tries as he plays through his day. Suddenly — out it comes!

NOVELS

Lafcadio, The Lion Who Shot Back - Shel Silverstein, Harper & Row, 1963.
Lafcadio's encounter with hunters turns him into the world's best shot. He becomes famous and takes on many human qualities, but he is not happy.

The Littles - John Peterson; Scholastic, Inc.; 1967.
The Littles are small people who live in the walls of the Biggs' house. When the Biggs rent their house, adventures follow.

The One In The Middle Is The Green Kangaroo - Judy Blume, Dell, 1981.
Being the middle child, Freddy feels left out of everything. The chance he finds to prove he's special shows everyone, including himself, that he is special.

Ramona And Her Father - Beverly Cleary, Morrow, 1975.
Ramona helps when her father loses his job, but everything she does bothers him. If only she could do something to make him happy again!

The Stories Julian Tells - Ann Cameron, Pantheon, 1981.
Some of Julian's stories get him into trouble, especially when younger brother Huey believes them — but sometimes Julian believes them, too.